Like Father Like Son

Like Father
Like Son

The Story of
Malcolm and Donald Campbell

by Phil Drackett

CLIFTON BOOKS

New England House, New England Street, Brighton BN1 4HN

Registered Office :
Clifton House, 83-117 Euston Road, London N.W.1.

First published 1969

Copyright © *Phil Drackett*

Printed in Great Britain
STRANGE THE PRINTER LIMITED, EASTBOURNE, SUSSEX

Contents

Illustrations

Prologue

These were the men

THE WORLD LAND SPEED RECORD requires the minimum of skill, the maximum of courage. Grand Prix motor racing requires tremendous skill and knowledge but also a refusal to be frightened.

These are the words of Tommy Wisdom, journalist, bon viveur, racing and rally driver, and not only a friend of both Malcolm and Donald Campbell but an active participant in their record-breaking activities.

Few men knew both father and son intimately apart from their immediate family and the ever-faithful Leo Villa. One of those was Tommy Wisdom. What impression of the Campbells has been left with him?

Perhaps the most abiding impression is that neither achieved what he wanted. Malcolm, the father, gained both land and water speed records but he badly wanted the air speed record too. By the time he had gathered the records on land and water others had put the air record far beyond his reach.

Donald, the son, always wanted to emulate his father. At a Brooklands meeting they turned up dressed in similar fashion, both smoking a pipe and both on motor-cycles. The effect was spoilt by the motor-bikes falling over after they had been carefully parked.

Yet the achievements of both represented a very special kind of courage.

Thus Tommy Wisdom.

Tommy and his wife 'Bill', lap record holder at the famous Brooklands track, not only knew Malcolm well but, of course, raced against him on many occasions.

Though Tommy would be the last to deny that Malcolm Campbell was a mercurial character, most of his recollections of the man are, nevertheless, happy ones. One shared experience was when they went on a voyage together on the *Aquitania* (1931 as Tommy remembers). There was some trouble with the rudder and the ship went around in circles. Tommy, then working for the *Daily Herald*, sent the story back. But it never reached his paper. The captain had apparently decided to impose his own censorship.

At about the same time, there was another occasion when Tommy, as one of Britain's leading motoring correspondents, found himself in trouble while covering a Campbell story. Malcolm was at Daytona Beach in the USA for a land record attempt, and for various reasons the bid was delayed. Tommy and a number of other correspondents cabled the news back to London. Mayor Armstrong of Daytona next heard from one of the British writers that a story had appeared in the London press to the effect that Campbell's bid had been delayed because the driver himself was 'windy'. The author of the story, said the mayor's informant, was one Tommy Wisdom.

The indignant mayor told Malcolm about this and cabled to J. S. Elias (later Lord Southwood), creator of the Odhams newspaper empire and the final arbiter on matters concerning the *Daily Herald*, demanding a retraction. The sequel was short. Elias cabled back that he had full confidence in Wisdom. Mayor Armstrong presented Wisdom with a case of Scotch. Malcolm Campbell and Tommy Wisdom remained on the best of terms.

Another incident concerning Malcolm and the press which Tommy recalls happened in 1929 when Malcolm's Bugatti burned out. A lad, now a distinguished motoring writer, had been sent to assist a leading correspondent in his coverage of the race. The lad was despatched to secure an interview with Malcolm on the disaster which had befallen him. He turned in a wonderful story—vivid descriptive writing which really put the reader in the place of the hapless Campbell as his car went up in flames and smoke.

A little later, the lad was walking along the pit area with his chief. A driver in overalls was lounging against the pit counter. 'Who's that?' queried the lad. 'You should know,' said his boss, 'that's Malcolm Campbell.'

Malcolm Campbell had his critics yet he was the first in line if an essential job had to be done. When war came in 1939, he tried, with the aid of W. A. Mackenzie, motoring correspondent of the *Daily Mail* and later the *Daily Telegraph*, and Tommy Wisdom, to form a Motor Cycle Corps. The scheme fell through but, says Tommy, it was typical of the attitude of the man to life's problems.

Donald, the son, was very different in some ways. He was intensely superstitious. His father may have been ('although if he was, I never realized it,' says Tommy) but Donald most certainly was. Stories that on the night before his death he drew the ace of spades in a card game, the 'Death Card', and was visibly affected, have been argued about in print but Tommy believes them. He recalls an incident on the ill-fated 1960 land speed record attempt. Donald was not an experienced car-driver like his father and an E-type Jaguar was brought down from Los Angeles, 750 miles away, so that he might gain experience of how to handle a fast car in a slide on the salt flats. When the Jag arrived it was found to be painted green. Donald, who firmly believed green to be an unlucky colour, refused to drive it. In this, perhaps, son was like father, bearing in mind the preference Malcolm had always shown for his cars and boats to be painted blue.

The night before the 1960 crash, Donald said he would like to change the foot-accelerator on *Bluebird* for a hand-throttle similar to the one used on the speed boats. Leo Villa and Tommy Wisdom dissuaded him. That decision may well have saved Donald's life. When the crash came, there could well have been an explosion had the hand-throttle been in operation keeping the engine at full revs. As it was, Donald's foot came off the conventional accelerator and the engine just kept ticking over—if you can say that a turbine just ticks over.

After the crash, doctors at the local hospital, accustomed

to dealing with the 'hot-rodders' who were their frequent guests, thought that Donald could be 'back on the track in two days'. Tommy insisted that a specialist be called and one was flown in from Los Angeles. He diagnosed a fractured skull.

These then were incidents which dotted the recollection of one man as he talked about the days when he raced against and worked with Donald and Malcolm Campbell. The legacy they left the world, he thinks, was courage. 'After all,' says Tommy Wisdom, 'record-breaking on land or water is just like a game of Russian roulette and any moment the loaded chamber may be the one aimed at your head.'

Chapter One

The End—and the Beginning

JANUARY 4TH, 1967. The turmoil of the waters subsided almost as quickly as it began. Soon only the breeze scuffed the surface, the breeze and the boats, their occupants vainly scanning the dark depths for something, anything, which might give a faint flicker of hope.

In a few brief minutes a world had changed, a story which had spanned more than 80 years had suddenly and devastatingly ended. For nine weeks, Donald Campbell and his team had been at Coniston Water in the Lake District awaiting a favourable moment for Campbell to attempt to break his own world water speed record of 276.33 mph and raise the figure above the 300 mph barrier. That morning the decision had been taken and about ten to nine Campbell started the mighty power unit of the fastest boat the world had ever seen, his $2\frac{1}{2}$-ton *Bluebird*. The silence was shattered as officials, mechanics, reporters and photographers, who had lived in a sort of twilight existence during the long weeks of waiting, suddenly realized, 'This is it'.

Campbell, tense and grim-faced, shrugged into the cockpit and the cover closed over his head. The giant craft nosed across the waters of the lake. To break the record, a timed run had to be completed in each direction within an hour.

Campbell opened up. *Bluebird* lifted, accelerated, 100 to 150 to 200 to 250. As she flashed over the measured kilometre, the official timekeeper radioed, 'Plus 47'. That meant 297 miles per hour, 21 mph faster than Campbell's existing record and within easy sight of the magic 300.

At the south end of the lake, which is nearly six miles long, Campbell turned and headed back for the second run. A speed of 303 mph on the return journey would be sufficient for him to reach his target, more than enough to smash his own record.

'Here we go'—his voice crackled faintly over the communication system. 'She's tramping slightly . . .', 'the water is not good . . .' Faster, faster, the boat hit the measured kilometre, accelerating all the time, faster, faster. Then, as the horrified watchers stood transfixed, 'She is going—I am on my back'. Like a dolphin rising from the surface of the sea, *Bluebird* soared nearly sixty feet into the air, somersaulted on to her back and, in a flurry of spume and spray, disappeared into the grim waters below. Within seconds there was no trace save a few air bubbles on the surface.

Campbell had been 200 yards from his greatest triumph and vindication, 200 yards from the record he so coveted. Chief Observer Norman Buckley, himself a speedboat record-breaker of no mean ability, said afterwards:

'Donald could have beaten his own record of 276 mph and reached the 300 mph average easily. He had only to return at 303 mph because his first run was completed at 297 mph. There can only be one reason for the tragedy. The boat was going so fast that it just took off. I estimate the speed on the return run at the time of the crash as between 310 and 320 mph.'

Whatever the reason for the disaster—and the discussions and the arguments were to continue for a long time—it brought to an end the most fantastic story in the annals of record-breaking.

It was still not one o'clock.

That was the end of the story.

This was the beginning.

On March 11th, 1885, at Chislehurst, Kent, the wife of a successful business-man, William Campbell, gave birth to a son, Malcolm. Despite the Kent domicile, the family originated from the Highlands. William's great-grandfather Andrew had taken the long road south to London and had built up a successful business as a jeweller and diamond merchant.

His sons and grandsons were to inherit his native shrewdness. When he retired, around 1838, he handed over the business to his son Joseph. Joseph had four sons, one of whom, another Andrew, maintained the commercial success of the family. He was followed by his second son, William, the same

William who had just been given a son and heir. Biographers have described William as a strict, hard and stern man. Certainly he continued the family tradition of being a good business-man, and when he died, some thirty-five years after Malcolm's birth, he left about a quarter of a million pounds, a sum by no means undesirable today and worth a great deal more then.

The infant 'mewling and puking' in his fond mother's arms was destined, however, to give the family traditions a shake-up. Heredity dies hard and there is little doubt that Malcolm the man inherited much of the family business instinct and ability to make money. But stronger than this in his make-up was a thirst for adventure, a throwback to the spirit which prompted great-great-grandfather Andrew to leave the grey, misty fastnesses of the Highlands for the cobbled-with-gold lanes and alleys of the City of London.

The adventurous streak in Malcolm led to many clashes of will and temperament with his father who was definitely—and not unexpectedly—Victorian in his outlook and had strong views on bringing up children. So those young years were a kaleidoscope of harum-scarum adventures, interviews with a stern parent and, eventually, sojourns in Egypt, Germany and France designed to complete Master Campbell's education and fit him to take over the family business in the fullness of time. Father, alas, was due for a shock!

Years afterwards Malcolm was to confess that the pattern of his life was set by an incurable thirst for speed. He could not explain it, he did not know what caused it. He only knew it was there and, like a disease, this thirst grew and grew.

Even on a pedal-cycle, he did his best to satisfy his longing. So much so that at Bromley Police Court he was charged with having driven a bicycle to the danger of the public, the prosecuting constable alleging that he had ridden down Bickley Hill at 27 miles per hour 'to the confusion and terror of two elderly ladies'.

Fining him thirty shillings, the magistrate uttered these words of admonition: 'Malcolm Campbell, you have endangered life and property on the public highway. You drove this machine of yours at a totally unnecessary speed. If you come before us again, we will take a much more serious view of the matter. We hope this will be a lesson to you not to travel so fast in future.' If he was still alive when Malcolm Campbell became the first man to set the world land speed record at over 300 mph, that magistrate's thoughts might have been interesting to record.

Those were the pioneer days of motoring, and for an adventurous lad like Malcolm it was not surprising that when the time came to decide his future he had vague leanings towards the infant motor trade. It was even less surprising that father William would not hear of it. He was determined that his son should have sound commercial training and the outcome was apprenticeship to an insurance broker. Although Malcolm did not realize it at the time, it was to lay the foundation of a business career which would give him the wherewithal to try to satisfy his desire for speed.

He found that insurance was a more interesting occupation than he had anticipated and eventually went into partnership in an underwriting syndicate. It was hard going at first but then the fledgling firm moved into the virgin field of libel insurance and success became assured. One account was with one of the biggest newspaper and magazine publishing groups in the country and financially the future began to look bright.

Around this time, an even more significant event took place. For fifteen pounds, Malcolm bought a second-hand Rex motor-cycle. Later he had a severe crash with it but not before he had been shown the way to satisfy the speed-urge within him. That Rex two-wheeler was the start of Campbell's life-long love affair with motor-cycles, cars and speedboats and even aeroplanes: a love affair which took precedence over everything else in his life and which, many years later, was to lead his own son to a rendezvous on Coniston Water.

Merely owning a motor-cycle was not enough. Soon he began to enter for the long-distance reliability trials which were then, in the early part of the twentieth century, much in vogue. He not only entered but acquitted himself well, and awards and medals came his way from such events as the

London—Exeter, London—Edinburgh and London—Land's End Trials.

Two wheels usually lead to four, but although Campbell's business was prospering modestly, car-owning in those days was only for men of considerable substance. The careers of many great men have hinged on the right opportunity coming along at the right time and it was just at this moment that a stroke of fortune came Campbell's way. He had made the acquaintance of an elderly and wealthy man who had expressed a great interest in Campbell's motor-cycling endeavours. The old gentleman commissioned Campbell to buy him a motor-car, with the one proviso that Campbell taught his patron to drive.

This was not so simple a condition as it sounded, for, despite his experience with motor-cycles, Malcolm had never been at the controls of a car! But to someone as resourceful as he this was the mildest of deterrents. He tracked down a suitable car, purchased it on behalf of his client, had five minutes' tuition from a mechanic and proceeded to give the new owner his first driving lesson. Surely quite enough to make present-day officials of the Ministry of Transport and the Royal Society for the Prevention of Accidents turn grey overnight!

In those days, however, there was more risk of collision with horses than with other motor-cars and the two intrepid 'autocarists' got away with it, although it is doubtful if the old chap, blissfully receiving 'expert' tuition from the 'experienced' driver beside him, ever knew the chance he was taking. The success of this mission led to someone else asking Malcolm to obtain a car for him and then to his acquiring the very first car of his own, a Panhard which was to be the forerunner of many.

The way ahead was not yet clearly defined and Campbell's interests were suddenly diverted from cars to other spheres. These were pioneer days too in the air and his enthusiasms changed direction. Big money prizes were being offered for achievements in 'flying machines' and Campbell turned all his energies, time and money to building his own aircraft.

The energy and the enthusiasm lasted a long time. The money and the aircraft unfortunately did not. The maiden flight of the 'do-it-yourself' craft ended in disaster in a field near Orpington. Rebuilt and offered for sale, the aircraft realized so little that Campbell found himself, temporarily at least, financially embarrassed. He turned back to motor-cycles and cars. Had he not done so, the history of the world's land-speed and water-speed records would have been very different. Now he put flying behind him.

He had already made his racing debut, on both two wheels and four, at the newly opened Brooklands track. The world had remained unimpressed. He now looked around for a car which would satisfy his demands and thus found himself the owner of an 80 mph Darracq.

This was, according to some sources, the car which had finished third in the Royal Automobile Club's Tourist Trophy Race of 1908, a race which for some reason had attracted the wrath of the press, led by *The Times*, which campaigned for its abandonment, claiming that death and destruction would result. There was a deliciously ironic sequel. *The Times* correspondent travelled by horse-and-cart to cover the race, the horse bolted and *The Times* man was thrown out, fortunately without serious injury. It is not recorded if *The Times* later campaigned for the abolition of horses and carts!

The race itself provided a thrilling struggle with Watson (Hutton) the winner from Algy Lee Guinness (Darracq) and the dashing Newcastle driver, A. E. George, in another car of the same make. George, in fact, was unlucky not to win, being robbed of victory by a six-minute delay when his car caught fire.

It was this car, then, that came into Campbell's possession, his first real racing-car. He too was to know what it meant to leap out of his machine in the middle of a race and try to extinguish the flames; but that lay many years in the future.

For the moment, he had obtained a very sound car with which to further his racing career. George had set the fastest lap in the TT with a speed of 52 mph and had covered the 340 miles of the twisting Isle of Man circuit at an average speed of 48 mph, a remarkable performance.

Campbell's early racing career at Brooklands has been partially obscured. In his book *The Lure of Speed* he says that in the first Darracq he owned he finished first and second in races at Brooklands. Dorothy Lady Campbell in her book, *Malcolm Campbell—The Man As I Knew Him* confirms this and adds that the car was, in fact, the TT Darracq. On the other hand, Bill Boddy, recognized as an authority on Brooklands, says in his encyclopaedic history of the track that Campbell failed to finish in two appearances in a Darracq but, after a spell with a Lion-Peugeot, later reappeared with the TT Darracq and was 'reasonably successful'.

That is a little mystery for the 'auto buffs' to puzzle over. What was to have more lasting significance was the naming of these early Campbell cars. At the time it was the fashion at Brooklands for drivers to give their cars nicknames and Campbell followed suit. His first two Darracqs and the Lion-Peugeot were all called *The Flapper* after a famous race-horse. One night a friend told Campbell of a play then running in London, Maurice Maeterlinck's *The Blue Bird*. For some reason the name fascinated the young racing-driver and—never one to let an enthusiasm pass unheeded—he knocked up the owner of a paint shop, dashed home and proceeded to paint blue the car he was to drive at Brooklands on the morrow. This was the third Darracq to come into his possession and he christened her *Bluebird*, a name which was to be handed on to every succeeding racing-car he owned, to his record-breaking cars and boats and then to the cars and boats driven by his son Donald. Rightly or wrongly, Campbell felt that the change of name and colour had also changed his racing luck for the better.

The first *Bluebird*, long since eclipsed in the history books by its many illustrious successors, was quite a remarkable car in its own right. It had been specially built for the big American race, the Vanderbilt Cup of 1909, and had a very powerful engine (165 mm bore × 140 mm stroke). It was capable of over 100 mph. Campbell bought it in 1911—wooden wheels, loose spokes, canvas tyres, heavy steering and all. Some engine tuning, a coat of paint, a new name—and who is to say which played the most important part?—and he proceeded to win races with it. He also had an extremely narrow escape from death when a front tyre burst just as he was entering the finishing straight at Brooklands at over 100 mph. The car skidded, Campbell straightened it out and hit the concrete kerb at the edge of the track. The front wheel on which the tyre had burst was smashed and as the car continued its course the rear wheel on the same side, the offside, also hit the kerb and broke into little pieces. Campbell yanked the steering-wheel hard over to the nearside and the car skidded sideways on a more or less straight course down the finishing straight, eventually coming to rest just a few inches from some railings behind which spectators were gathering.

The latter seemed so mesmerized by the whole performance that none of them took steps to scuttle away to safety. It was a near squeak for all of them. Amongst the spectators was a motoring journalist and his daughter, Dorothy. Introduced to Campbell after his narrow escape by her father, Dorothy was much impressed with the racing-driver. It was to be a fateful meeting for both of them.

So the curtain went up on the *Bluebird* story as it was to end, on a note of high drama. The drama was not confined to Campbell's deeds on the track but spilled over into his personal life. In 1913 he married for the first time. His wife had considerable money of her own and being keenly interested in Campbell's motor-racing exploits was only too willing to help him financially in building up his stable of cars. It was she too who bought him his first motor-boat, which awoke in him the urge for speed on water as well as on land. But in other respects it was not a happy marriage and it was doomed to failure and eventual divorce.

Nor were the domestic clouds the only ones looming on the horizon. The day before the Great War began, Campbell drove in the last race of the final Brooklands meeting of 1914. Next day Campbell set off for France as one of the Royal Automobile Club's squad of volunteer car owner-drivers. Not only did these motoring pioneers offer their services but they took their own cars with them to place at the disposal of the British Army.

It was too much to expect that someone of Malcolm's temperament would be content to chauffeur staff officers around behind the lines. He transferred to the infantry and then, in 1915, to the Royal Flying Corps. Oddly enough, in the light of his subsequent exploits, it was decided that he was too ham-fisted to be a fighter-pilot and he spent most of the war firstly ferrying planes across the Channel and then as an instructor, eventually becoming a captain and being awarded the MBE.

So for five long years motor-racing was but a memory. With the coming of peace, 34-year-old Malcolm Campbell was about to write the first chapter of the *Bluebird* story proper, a story which was to make front-page headlines for nearly five decades, to involve the expenditure of millions of pounds, bring decorations and awards and make Great Britain pre-eminent in the world of record-breaking.

Chapter Two

The Stage Is Set

MALCOLM CAMPBELL RETURNED FROM THE WAR to find his insurance underwriting business still prospering and he himself assured of a good income with a minimum of effort. His restless mind therefore turned in other directions. He went into the motor-trade, a somewhat ill-fated venture with which we need not concern ourselves here, save to say that car historians may care to note that at one time there was a car on the market known as the Gregoire-Campbell, a famous Continental car with Campbell's name added to strengthen his role of London agent. The Gregoire-Campbell did not sell well. Nor did its successor in the Campbell showrooms, the Mors.

On the face of it, an agency for Mors should have been a passport to fortune. One of the outstanding French marques (and it must be remembered that although the Germans deserve most of the credit for 'inventing' the motor-car it was the French who developed and exploited it), Mors had galloped away with a major share of honours in the early days of motor-racing. It included victories in the 1899 Paris—St. Malo and Bordeaux—Biarritz events; an unofficial and moral victory in the 1900 Gordon-Bennett race with Levegh at the controls; and unchallenged triumph in the 1901 Paris—Berlin and Paris—Bordeaux races, with Fournier at the helm. Moreover, everyone had heard of Mors when Fernand Gabriel won the notorious 'Race of Death' from Paris to Madrid in 1903, the race being halted at Bordeaux because of the many accidents. Nothing could disguise the fact that the Mors driven by Gabriel covered 342¾ miles in 5 hours 13 minutes and 31.5 seconds, an average speed of over 65 mph.

Despite this, and despite the story that the Mors victory in the 1901 Paris—Berlin race had been worth twenty million francs in orders to the factory, Malcolm found that in the post-world-war period the name of Mors meant little—at least to that small minority of the British public which had money enough to contemplate the purchase of an automobile. It perhaps has some significance to later events, however, that on several occasions in the early history of the automobile, the world land speed record had been held by Mors cars.

What might have made money for Malcolm and sent his footsteps up another road was an early tie-up with a man called William Morris, later to become Lord Nuffield. However, they failed to see eye-to-eye—not unnaturally for two men of such strong and contrasting personalities—and what might well have been a most remarkable combination never really got into its stride.

Despite the complications of motor trading, Malcolm's insurance income guaranteed that he had time and money to satisfy his love for speed. He went all over the British Isles to compete in hill-climbs, usually most successfully, and he was one of the first on parade when Brooklands reopened in 1920. The track had been repaired after the ravages of war-time use, petrol rationing had ended, there were plenty of cars available and a full season's racing was envisaged.

The inaugural meeting was held in April and organized by the Essex Motor Club. The very first post-war race was won by Campbell's pre-war 2.6-litre Talbot at an average speed of 84.5 mph.

For the first big event of the season, the Easter meeting, organized by the British Automobile Racing Club, Campbell trotted out his latest pride, a 1912 15-litre Lorraine-Dietrich which had taken part in the French Grand Prix and later broke records in the hands of Victor Hemery. Campbell had acquired it in France and his adventures in getting past Customs with the car make quite a story in themselves.

He discovered the car in Paris during his war service, bought it and then found to his dismay that the import of foreign cars into the UK was forbidden. He hit upon the idea of telling His Majesty's Customs that the car had been used for staff duties on the Western Front but found himself up against a somewhat cynical Customs officer. That seemed to settle the matter, but the one consistent trait in Malcolm Campbell's life was a refusal ever to be beaten, and eventually the Lorraine-Dietrich, known as *Vieux Charles Troix*, found itself at Brooklands.

Unfortunately, rain interfered with the Easter programme, but Campbell ran a match race against Major Woodhouse's Matchless motor-cycle and won at 78.9 mph. Lest you think this a quaint idea of the twenties—car against motor-cycle—a similar project was seriously advocated for the Isle of Man in the sixties with the names of John Surtees and Mike Hailwood mentioned as possible contestants. Thirty or forty years ago, such contests were quite common.

Campbell sold the Lorraine and bought a Schneider which he thought was faster. He promptly had the mortification of seeing the Lorraine put up some fine winning performances with other people at the wheel. Most races at Brooklands were, of course, run under handicap and the race was not always to the most swift.

Just the same, there were portents of coming events. Driving a 1912 7.6-litre Grand Prix Peugeot, Malcolm collected a stack of class records over distances from half-mile to ten miles, his speed over the half being over 109 mph.

It had not been a sensational year, either for Brooklands or for Campbell, but at least motor-racing was under way again and the names of many of those who had competed during the season gave out great promise for the future. Amongst them were Douglas Hawkes, Henry Segrave, Archie Frazer-Nash, C. M. Harvey, Kensington Moir, Harry Hawker (whose true fame lay in the air) and that remarkable woman driver, Violet Cordery.

The following year saw the boom (if that it can be called) really under way with many names which were to be headline news throughout the twenties and thirties appearing at Brooklands. A fleeting appearance on the scene was made by a young man named 'Tim' Birkin who, after a rather mild debut in a DFP, was to disappear for six long years before returning in triumph as one of the never-to-be-forgotten

'Bentley Boys' who swept all before them at Le Mans and gained Britain her only major motoring successes in a long time.

Start of the 1921 season was the Easter meeting at which Malcolm Campbell had entered his pre-war 2.6-litre Talbot. In the 3-litre scratch race, a new event, this car finished second but a long, long way behind Henry Segrave in a prototype Sunbeam. Again coming events were casting their shadow before, since Segrave was to score Britain's only Grand Prix successes of the 'between wars' period, driving for the Sunbeam 'works' team.

Campbell also finished second in the Junior 2-mile Sprint, the race being won by Cocker driving a Crouch, both names which have long since faded into limbo. Campbell got into winning form at the Whitsun meeting and took the first race of the day, the 100 mph Short Handicap, from Noble (AC) and McVicar (Waverley). To do this Campbell beat his handicap by exactly five miles per hour on his fastest lap. The eye-catchers were, however, the big cars, Zborowski's Mercedes and Segrave's Sunbeam, but they found their handicap too much despite clocking well over the ton on their fastest laps. The Senior Sprint Handicap found Campbell in second place again, the winner being King in a new Austin Twenty.

Malcolm entered two cars for the mid-summer meeting, a Talbot, powered by a 4½-litre engine which had once reposed in Percy Lambert's 1913 record-breaking car, and a 3½-litre Mors. He was, of course, selling Mors cars in his London showrooms and was convinced that racing success led to improved sales of domestic vehicles.

Certainly the racing cars of those days provided a weird assortment. There were plenty of cars primarily built for racing and record-breaking but also a number—almost in the family saloon or town carriage class—which had been tuned by their enthusiastic owners to deeds which would have made the manufacturers shudder. Cars in this category at the mid-summer meeting included a Rolls-Royce with touring body and an Armstrong-Siddeley two-seater, complete with dickey-seat. Of more significance was Lionel Martin's Aston Martin, a car which was to play a major role in motor sport for years to come.

It was not a very good meeting as far as Campbell was concerned and he was forced to retire the Talbot in the 100 mph Long Handicap. The August meeting was much better for him, the Talbot finishing third in the 100 mph Short Handicap, although Malcolm can hardly have been overjoyed since the winner was Douglas Hawkes in the Lorraine-Dietrich which had once been his.

The Talbot was a very reliable car, however, and, although unplaced, lapped at more than 83 mph in the 75 mph Short Handicap. Once again the handicap was too much for the fastest car in the race and the ubiquitous Cocker in his Crouch was the winner, but Campbell rounded off the day by finishing second in the Junior Sprint.

Two victories came Malcolm's way at the autumn meeting. In the 4½-litre Talbot he won the 100 mph Long Handicap and in his smaller car of the same make took the 75 mph Long Handicap at 83.19 mph. Bearing in mind this all happened nearly fifty years ago, there were some fantastic performances in these two races. The Austin Twenty finished second to Campbell in the '100' and lapped at 94.5 mph, whilst the Straker-Squire in third place did its last lap at 103.11 mph. In the '75', Waite's Austin clocked more than 90 mph.

Racing and record-breaking continued at the Weybridge track throughout the year, even in the winter months, and as the year faded, Kaye Don in an AC captured many Light Car class records. Don, like Campbell, had a role to play in the forthcoming world land speed bids which were to capture public imagination through the twenties and thirties—although, unlike Campbell, success would elude him.

Campbell himself was already beginning to harbour thoughts of record-breaking, but for the moment racing and hill-climbing dominated his activities. He still retained the big Talbot for the 1922 Brooklands season but had sold the 2.6-litre Talbot to Woolf Barnato, another of the famous 'Bentley Boys'. Another car which had formerly belonged to Malcolm, the Schneider, was now in the hands of Le Champion.

A newcomer on the scene was Parry Thomas with a Leyland Eight and he too was destined to make his mark on the world land speed record. Before that, however, he would sweep the board at Brooklands and become the most successful driver in the long history of that famous circuit.

The winners' list at the Easter meeting which started the 1922 Brooklands season read like a rollcall of the great.

Just look:

Easter Private Competitors' Handicap:
  Count Zborowski (Ballot) 101 mph.
Scratch Light Car Race:
  Kaye Don (AC) 89.5 mph.
Thirteenth Lightning Short Handicap:
  Jean Chassagne (Sunbeam) 103.75 mph.
100 mph Short Handicap Race:
  Kaye Don (AC) 92 mph.
90 mph Short Handicap:
  Malcolm Campbell (Talbot) 87.38 mph.
Lightning Long Handicap:
  Ernest Eldridge (Isotta-Fraschini) 100 mph.
90 mph Long Handicap:
  Malcolm Campbell (Talbot) 89 mph.
75 mph Long Handicap:
  Marshall (Hampton) 76.03 mph.
100 mph Long Handicap:
  Count Zborowski (Ballot) 106.88 mph.

Just as a reminder of the fallibility of great drivers and great cars, the 75 mph Short Handicap was won by a Crouch, this one driven by Tollady. The Crouch was certainly an odd-looking car and was chain-driven. This particular example must have looked especially horrible as it was painted primrose yellow. It lapped at 73.13 mph which, on handicap, was good enough to keep it ahead of Bedford's Hillman which was lapping at 84.27 mph. Some Brooklands drivers of the period must have thought the handicapper a rather harsh man.

For the May meeting, Malcolm Campbell produced his 1912 Grand Prix Peugeot, *Bluebird*, and put up an excellent performance in the 90 mph Long Handicap, clocking a race average of 103.11 mph. It earned him only second place because for once Bedford, far from leniently treated though he

was, managed to beat the handicapper and win the race at
83.87 mph.

Malcolm was not in the winning lists for the next two
meetings, one a royal occasion attended by the Duke of York
and the other the customary Whitsun meeting, at which he
was entered in a 1½-litre Austro-Daimler. Zborowski, Parry
Thomas and Barnato were all amongst the victors. Nor did
August Bank Holiday bring better luck although Campbell
drove three different cars: the Luther-entered Austro-Daimler,
the 1912 Peugeot and the Whittall-entered FIAT.

However, on the record-breaking front all sorts of things
happened at Brooklands that year, some of which were to
figure largely in Malcolm Campbell's future. Kaye Don went
on breaking class records, the Aston Martin team smashed
no less than 32 records in one go and, most significant of all,
Kenelm Lee Guinness broke the world land speed record. Of
that we shall have much more to say later. For the moment,
suffice it to say that Campbell looked at Lee Guinness's
Sunbeam and wanted it—very much—for his own.

The young motor-racing enthusiast of today may be
surprised to know that bookmakers enlivened the Brooklands
scene and one of them issued a card of 'owners' colours' in
which Malcolm Campbell was allocated tartan. The tartan
was soon to score a victory when the 1923 season opened. In
many ways this year was a milestone in Campbell's life.
Although he would continue to compete in motor-races for
many years to come, from now on record-breaking would be
his main interest, his all-absorbing passion, the secure rock on
which his fame would rest.

First of all, there were races to be won. In an event for 'the
big boys', *Bluebird* averaged 92.25 mph to take the 100 mph
Long Handicap. This race must have provided an awe-
inspiring sight with Le Champion clocking 111.17 mph in the
giant Isotta. Campbell, in the winning *Bluebird*, reached
101.43 mph, and followed up with a second victory in the
90 mph Short Handicap, his Ballot averaging 82.63 mph.

In passing, the private competitors' race was won by a
gentleman named Alfred Moss whose son, Stirling by name,

later did a bit of racing! The small car race provided the first-ever win for what became one of the world's most famous cars, the Austin Seven.

Malcolm's next Brooklands win was delayed until the August meeting when he was first in the 90 mph Long Handicap, driving a Ballot which, like the Peugeot, was named *Bluebird*. Then at the autumn meeting, at the wheel of an Itala (for he was nothing if not versatile), he once more won the 90 mph Long Handicap and finished second in the 90 mph Short to Clement's Bentley.

Campbell also started the 1924 Brooklands season with a victory, winning the 75 mph Short Handicap at the Easter meeting in a Star. He followed up by taking the Lightning Long Handicap in his newly acquired Sunbeam and later in the year at the summer meeting won the 100 Long in his Ballot and the 75 Long in the Itala. Then in August he was triumphant in the Lightning Long, once again at the wheel of the Sunbeam. Just to share the honours around amongst his cars, he took the 75 Short at the autumn meeting in the Star.

It had proved to be his best season so far, yet already his record-breaking activities were overlapping his racing ventures. It had been a turbulent year at Brooklands. There were complaints from local residents about the noise and then tragedy befell when Captain Toop was killed at the Whitsun meeting and the veteran international racing driver, Dario Resta, a naturalized Briton, met with a fatal accident whilst attempting records in September. It seems an appropriate moment to pause in the story of Campbell's exploits and take a look at the world land speed record which was soon to become his main purpose in life.

Chapter Three

The World Land Speed Record

WHAT WAS THE MAGNITUDE OF THE TASK Malcolm Campbell was about to set himself? What, indeed, was the world land speed record?

Officially there was no such animal. The International Automobile Federation recognized what were known as International Class Records, covering nearly all sizes of engines, distances and durations. The fastest of these records was popularly known as the 'world land speed record' and from the pioneer days of motoring it was this unofficial title which captured the imagination of the public and the ambitions of drivers, designers and mechanics.

Since it is obviously easier (although the word can only be used comparatively) to achieve the greatest speeds over the shortest distances, attempts on the 'heavyweight championship' of motor sport were usually made over a flying kilometre or flying mile or both.

In an age when electric cars have their advocates as the town runabouts of the future, it is perhaps ironical that the first car to hold the world land speed record was electric, the early history of the record being a nip-and-tuck battle between cars powered in this fashion. The honour of being the first title-holder went rather appropriately to a Frenchman. Although the practical motor-car owes much to the Germans Daimler and Benz, it was the French who ran the first motor-races and set in train the world-wide growth of motoring. The French Automobile Club was the first ever to be founded (in 1895) and was followed two years later by the Automobile Club of Great Britain and Ireland, now the RAC.

One of the founder-members of the French club was the Marquis de Chasseloup-Laubat and it was he and his brother, the Comte Gaston de Chasseloup-Laubat, who essayed the first-ever attempt on the world record. The marquis had built an electric car, the Jeantaud, and a good stretch of road at Achéres, near Paris, was chosen for the bid. With Gaston as driver, the Jeantaud covered a kilometre at the then sensational speed of 39.24 mph.

The gauntlet had been thrown down—and there was soon a challenger to pick it up. The French brothers set the record in December 1898, and by January 1899 a red-bearded Belgian had appeared on the scene determined to wrest the honour from them. Camille Jenatzy, later to become famous as a very successful racing driver for the German Mercedes team, was at that time enthusiastic about becoming a large-scale manufacturer of electric cars.

He turned up at Achéres with a car of his own design and promptly proceeded to set a new record at 41.42 mph. It was a short-lived triumph since Gaston replied with 43.69 mph.

The Belgian took himself off to build bigger and better batteries for his car. Nothing loth to join battle, the Chasseloup brothers did likewise. Jenatzy was ready first and regained the record with 49.92 mph. This time Gaston made a decisive response and boosted the figure to no less than 57.60 mph, thus becoming the first man to achieve the 50 mph target.

So far the record attempts had been timed with somewhat primitive apparatus and by timekeepers who held no official status. Now, with interest rapidly increasing and the speeds rising sharply, the French Automobile Club decided it was time to step in, impose a set of rules and appoint official timekeepers.

At this point the Chasseloup brothers bowed out of the world record scene and, regrettably, have subsequently had less than their due from posterity. For it is the picturesque Belgian, Jenatzy, wearing what one historian has described as a 'villainous-looking fur coat', and his no less famous car, *La Jamais Contente*, on whom the spotlight of history has descended.

Not, of course, without justification. Under the new regime, Jenatzy with a revised version of his car—bigger and better batteries and motors—smashed the record at a speed of

65.79 mph. (This, remember, in 1899.) In so doing he set a
number of notable landmarks: the first man to travel at more
than 60 mph, a mile a minute; the first recorded vehicle to
make use of a torpedo-like shape which later became known as
stream-lining; and, although naturally no one realized it at the
time, the last electric car to hold the world land speed record.
Today, a speed of a mile a minute has no appreciable significance
for most of us, when many ordinary family saloons are capable
of 80 and 90 mph and fast train services doddle along at
100 mph (or at least are supposed to do). But in the fading
months of the nineteenth century many people believed that
no man could survive the effects on his breathing and nervous
system of travelling at such tremendous speeds. What would
they think of the American and Russian astronauts today?

After Jenatzy's wonderful record there was, perhaps not
surprisingly, a lull for a time until in 1902, with people still
talking fearfully about the dangers of such speeds, a steam car
demolished the record at 75.06 mph. The driver and designer
was a Frenchman, Leon Serpollet, and it is a tribute to his
engineering ability that some of his cars still take part in veteran
car runs and rallies today. The drawback of the electric car
was the necessity to charge the battery at regular intervals.
Steam too had grave handicaps. Instead of electric charges,
the steam car needed frequent water supplies. Moreover, it
also needed time to get up a full head of steam before setting
off on a run. These were difficulties which the dedicated
Serpollet shrugged aside and certainly he could be forgiven
for feeling on top of the world as he steamed along the Promen-
ade des Anglais at Nice at full throttle, the first man to achieve
another magic milestone, 75 mph.

However, the bell tolled not only for the electric car but for
the steam-car and the man who took the first heave on the
bell-rope was an American millionaire, W. K. Vanderbilt.
Destiny had marked him out as the first man to break the
world land speed record with a car powered by an internal
combustion engine—the first but most certainly not the last.
His initial attempt did not set the world on fire. Using a
Mercedes-Simplex, he clocked the exact speed at which

Jenatzy had last taken the record, good but nearly ten miles an hour slower than Serpollet's existing record. Millionaires are not usually thwarted easily, and four months later, in August 1902, Vanderbilt was ready for another shot at the record, this time at Ablis, near Chartres.

He chose a Paris-Vienna Mors, a car designed for road-racing and consequently carrying a lot of equipment extraneous to the business of record-breaking. Despite this the attempt succeeded and Vanderbilt became the new record-holder at 76.08 mph. Now the battle was really joined. Other drivers realized that cars like the Mors could be modified and improved strictly for record-breaking and soon Vanderbilt's record toppled to Henry Fournier in a similar Mors at 76.6 mph. Fournier held the record less than a month before Augières, also driving a Mors, bumped the figure up to 77.13 mph.

Next on the scene was *Gobbling Billie*, a giant 100 horse-power, Gobron-Brillie, driven by Arthur Duray. At Ostend in July 1903, Duray elevated the record to 83.47 mph and a few months later at Dourdan pushed it still higher to 84.73 mph. Meanwhile, in the United States, a gentleman named Henry Ford claimed a figure of 91.37 and Vanderbilt bobbed up again with a run of 92.30. These two runs put the cat amongst the pigeons. The Automobile Club of America was not recognized by the international controlling body, which consequently declined to recognize either achievement as a world record. It was an unsatisfactory state of affairs and there must have been relief, in European hearts at least, when in March 1904 *Gobbling Billie* reappeared, this time with Louis Rigolly at the controls, and beat official and unofficial records twice in one day, first at 93.20 mph and then at 94.78.

Baron Pierre de Caters soon snatched the record from Rigolly, driving his Gordon-Bennett Mercedes at a speed of 97.26 mph at Ostend. It was a year of triumph for the baron, who, even in 1904, could truthfully be described as a veteran racing driver, having been at it for some ten years. Not only did he take the world record but he also achieved his first major racing success by winning the Circuit des Ardennes.

Caters' record was clear indication that before long someone would reach the magic figure of 100 mph, and so it proved. The man to do it was Rigolly, the car the Gobron-Brillie which had already twice held the world record, the place Ostend and the speed 103.56 mph.

That was in July 1904, and in November the record passed to another 100 horse-power car, this time a Darracq, driven by P. Baras, winner of the 1899 Paris—Ostend Race. Baras succeeded only in increasing the figure to 104.53 mph and this record was soon under unofficial fire from the States where a young Englishman, Arthur Macdonald, clocked 104.65 in a Napier, and Herbert Bowden in a Mercedes-engined car registered 109.75 mph. The Americans recognized Macdonald's figures as a world record but not Bowden's, since his car exceeded the weight limit laid down for Grand Prix racing cars. The international authorities, of course, did not recognize either. Bowden's car, however, deserves more than a passing glance. It had a specially built long chassis with two 60 horse-power Mercedes engines set in tandem. In other words, it was the first internal-combustion-engined 'special' to appear in the world record lists and was the forerunner of many others. By the time Malcolm Campbell was to loom large on the record scene, record-breakers would all be 'specials'.

But that was still years in the future. For the moment, the scene returned to Europe where a new official record was set by Victor Hemery, driving a monster Darracq of 200 horse-power. His speed, on a stretch of road between Arles and Salon, was 109.65 mph, fractionally below Bowden's unofficial record.

Hemery, however, was about to beard the Americans in their own den and at the outset of 1906 took the Darracq to the Daytona Speed Trials. Fate had a surprise in store and one of the most dramatic and bizarre episodes in the annals of record-breaking was about to take place.

No playwright could have conceived a bigger surprise twist, no actor could ever have had a more dramatic final curtain. Hemery was not to retain the world record but no Vanderbilt, no Ford, no Bowden, was to wrest it from him.

The proud new record-holder was to be a steam car, a Stanley Steamer, driven by Frank Marriott. The chassis was

(above) A happy Malcolm Campbell waves to the crowd after becoming the first man to break the world land speed record at more than 200 mph: Daytona Beach, 1928. (*Photo by 'Planet News'*)

(below) Father and son. The young Donald Campbell talks with his father during preparation for a water speed attempt by Malcolm. (*Photo by R. S. Sanderson, Grasmere*)

Leo Villa, chief 'backroom boy' to both the Campbells, holds Donald's *Bluebird* steady at Lake Coniston. (*Photo by Geoff Hallawell*)

the standard 10 horse-power production model Stanley Steamer but incorporating a specially made boiler designed to withstand much higher pressures than normal. Encased in a streamlined body not so very dissimilar from the Grand Prix racing cars of today, Marriott became the first man to take the record at more than two miles a minute. His speed over the kilometre was 121.57 mph and for the mile 127.66. For some reason, the authorities in Paris chose to recognize only the lower speed. It was to be the last time a steam car held the record but what a swan-song it was. So magnificent was Marriott's achievement that nearly four years were to pass before his record was broken.

Even then, it was only the kilometre record which was broken with a speed of 125.95 mph. Hemery was the driver, this time in a Blitzen-Benz, and the venue was the Brooklands race track, which had been opened two years earlier, in 1907. Despite the controversy which this run has aroused in view of Marriott's figures, it is interesting to note that Hemery was timed at the half-mile at 127.887 mph, so the merit of his achievement is undeniable. It was notable in many ways: the first time the record had been set at Brooklands, the first time a petrol-engined car had taken the record at more than two miles per minute and the last time a record was permitted on the evidence of a run in one direction only. After this it was ruled that in future all short-distance records must be established on the mean time of two runs over the course, one in each direction.

Meanwhile, another disputed claim came from America where that larger-than-life personality, Barney Oldfield, clocked 131.72 mph at Daytona.

Four more years were to elapse before in 1914, on the eve of the world conflagration, a Briton, L. G. Hornsted, driving a colossal 21,504 cc Benz, became the first man to be recognized as the official world record-holder under the new rules requiring a run in each direction. His speed for the two runs was 124.10 mph but there was a satisfactory reply to those who pointed to Hemery's kilometre record because the faster of Hornsted's two runs was made at 128.16 mph. Duray made

C

an unsuccessful attempt on these figures with a FIAT at Ostend but war broke out with the record reposing at Brooklands.

The aftermath of war brought many problems—profiteers spending their profits, ex-officers losing their money in chicken farms, manufacturers building spidery little cycle-cars and the League of Nations building dreams at Geneva. But motor-racing, in Britain at least and thanks largely to Brooklands, was soon in full stride.

One of the fastest cars in existence at the time was an 18,322 cc Sunbeam which lapped Brooklands in 1921 at a speed of 120.01 mph. In May 1922, Kenelm Lee Guinness ('KLG' of sparking-plug fame) went all-out for the record and was timed over a kilometre at 133.75 mph, nearly ten miles an hour faster than Hornsted's 1914 record. That was the last seen of the world land speed record at Brooklands for the track just wasn't fast enough for the even more powerful record-breakers which were to follow in the wake of Lee Guinness and his Sunbeam.

The scene switched to Arpajon in France, and a two-way battle for the record between the Frenchman, René Thomas, and the Englishman, Ernest Eldridge. Eldridge had a FIAT powered with a 21-litre aircraft engine, and a fantastic sight it must have been as it snaked along the narrow course, Eldridge wrestling with the wheel, and his passenger (yes, he carried a passenger) hanging on for dear life. Eldridge's mean speed was 147.03 mph and it seemed that the world record was his when Thomas managed only 143.29 mph. But the Frenchman protested that Eldridge's car was not fitted with reverse gear as demanded by the regulations and Eldridge's figures were accordingly disallowed.

It availed the Frenchman little. Eldridge fitted a reverse mechanism of sorts and a week later clocked 146.01 mph in an attempt which was officially recognized. It was the last time the record was to be set on the road.

A new era was about to dawn with cars specially built for record-breaking and costing many, many thousands of pounds. The sea shores and deserts of the world would have to be surveyed to find suitable stretches where these monsters could be let out to their maximum speeds. Waiting in the wings to drive them were men like Parry Thomas, Ray Keech, Lee Bible, Frank Lockhart, George Eyston, John Cobb and Henry Segrave.

But the man who was to make the biggest imprint on the history of the world land speed record was Malcolm Campbell, and his appearance on the scene was not to be long delayed.

Chapter Four

If at first . . . .

THERE WAS NO DOUBT ABOUT IT, Kenelm Lee Guinness's achievement in May 1922 of capturing the world land speed record in a Sunbeam had fired new ambitions in Malcolm Campbell. He firmly believed that this car was the prototype of things to come, of cars which would revolutionize the racing and record-breaking worlds. He wanted that Sunbeam badly and he was determined to have it. Every time he met Louis Coatalen, the head of the Sunbeam Company, he offered to buy the car and every time Coatalen refused. But Campbell was a man of strong will and determination and at last Coatalen weakened to the extent of agreeing to loan him the car for speed trials which were to be held in June at Saltburn Sands, the meeting being organized by the Yorkshire Automobile Club.

Conditions were good, the sun shone, the sand was smooth and hard, and the Sunbeam had been specially tuned. Campbell clocked 130.6 mph in one direction over the measured mile and 134.08 in the other, and it was announced to the watching thousands that he had broken the mile record. Disappointment was to follow. The International Sporting Commission refused to recognize it as a record since hand-timing had been used and not electrical timing apparatus. Campbell was naturally upset but the setback only made him more determined than ever. Besides, not all the luck at Saltburn had been bad, for on his return run one of the local doggy inhabitants decided to take a stroll on the sands, right in the path of the Sunbeam. Campbell coolly calculated that collision would narrowly be avoided at his present speed providing the dog did not decide to turn back on his tracks. Fortunately the dog kept on walking and Campbell afterwards estimated that car and quadruped missed each other by a matter of some six feet. What the dog felt when a 150 mph missile exploded just behind his rear quarters is not recorded, but according to contemporary accounts our canine friend was last seen swimming strongly in the direction of Sweden.

The technicalities of timing could not disguise the fact that the Sunbeam was all that Campbell hoped. He renewed pressure on poor Mr. Coatalen to sell and eventually that worthy gentleman gave in, not one imagines without driving a fairly hard bargain for such a dream of a car. In the interim, the Danish Automobile Club had announced that it was to hold international speed trials at Fanoe Island in the spring of 1923 and the Sunbeam was duly entered. When the Sunbeam was delivered at Horley station (Campbell had by then married again—the girl he had met at Brooklands—and was living at Povey Cross) there was another big disappointment in store.

The car was driven from station to garage amid clouds of smoke and on inspection it was found that the scavenging pump had broken, oil thus being pumped from the tank into the sump but not returning. The car had in fact been standing at Brooklands more or less neglected since Malcolm had driven it at Saltburn the previous year. Although it was now Monday and the car had to leave for Denmark on Saturday, the difficulties did not seem insurmountable. Campbell had built an extremely well-equipped garage at the Povey Cross house and had three mechanics to assist him, one of them a Sunbeam-trained specialist who had been loaned by Coatalen to help prepare the car. They worked on it all the week and then, on Friday, decided to carry out a routine inspection of the gearbox. To their horror and dismay, they found three gears completely stripped. The shaft had been turned out of solid steel and there was not another one in existence.

All thought of entering the Danish trials must surely be abandoned. True, there was another steamer sailing on Monday which would reach Denmark in time, but how could the car possibly be repaired? A lesser man than Malcolm Campbell would have given a resigned shrug, told the mechanics to wheel the Sunbeam back into the garage and made plans for another day. Not he. Soon the wires were buzzing to the Sunbeam factory in Wolverhampton. Yes, they could machine a new shaft but the steel would have to be obtained from Sheffield. So the mechanic on loan from Sunbeam, an unsung hero named Webster, volunteered to drive to Sheffield, pick up the steel, deliver it to Wolverhampton, wait for the shaft to be machined and then go straight to Liverpool Street where the rest of the team, complete with wounded car, would be waiting at the boat-train. It does less than justice to a remarkable effort to record barely that Webster, shaft tucked under his arm, came sprinting along the platform at Liverpool Street just as the train was about to pull out.

Racing was due to begin on Saturday: they arrived on Tuesday and by sheer hard work had the car ready for testing on Friday. Then on its first test run, every one of the shock-absorber brackets broke. But no one had the slightest intention of giving up at that stage and the weary mechanics once again performed wonders to have the car ready in time.

For once, virtue had its own reward. In the standing mile, the Sunbeam easily defeated the German Opel with the rest of the international field nowhere. Then came the big event, the flying mile and kilometre, the distances over which the world land speed record centred. The Sunbeam recorded an average of 137.72 mph for the two runs while the Opel could manage only 132. Campbell thought the world record was his and proceeded to celebrate by winning the big car race which closed the meeting.

Fate, however, had once again some disappointment in store and again the International Sporting Commission were the 'villains' of the piece. They refused to allow the record because although electrical timing equipment had been used it was not of a type officially approved. The Danish Automobile Club protested and even went to the extent of sending the equipment to Paris where it was tested and found accurate. It was all in vain—no record for Campbell.

Looking back in after years, Dorothy Lady Campbell thought it probably a good thing for the future of the world land speed record. Had the authorities recognized his 1923 runs, she felt there was a distinct possibility that her husband would have given up further attempts although, in collaboration with Amherst Villiers, he had been preparing designs for a record-breaker which would be truly his own.

What might have been none of us will ever know, but Campbell was soon busily at work again and the Sunbeam blossomed forth in a new 'coat', a specially designed streamlined body built by Boulton & Paul, the aircraft manufacturers. The Danish speed trials were to be held again at Fanoe in 1924 and Malcolm was determined to be there. Meanwhile, of course, the world record had fallen to another British driver, Ernest Eldridge.

What happened on his second visit to Fanoe was almost enough to break Campbell's heart. He took every precaution possible, obtained permission for the British RAC's officially approved timing apparatus to be used and for the Brooklands Clerk of the Course and Official Timekeeper to be in charge of these aspects of the operation. Remembering the frantic struggle to be ready in time for the 1923 trials, he made sure that the whole team arrived in Denmark three days beforehand.

Yet after all this, after designing a new body, tuning the car thoroughly, checking the timing apparatus, taking every precaution possible, the attempt was to end again in failure and worse—dire tragedy which was to have a downcasting effect on everyone connected with the Sunbeam.

Storms had swept Denmark and the beach was not only in poor condition but littered with the debris of the sea. Although a narrow course was cleared it was hardly satisfactory and spectators were allowed to crowd up to the very edge. Warnings were uttered about the dangers but apparently no action was taken.

The Sunbeam had reached a speed of some 150 mph and was nearing the end of the measured mile when it began to slew sideways. Campbell fought to keep it straight, then saw something bounding beside the car. It was the offside front tyre!

Travelling at tremendous speed, the tyre hurtled into the crowd and hit a boy spectator. He died soon afterwards. The

meeting was abandoned and although Campbell and his team
were absolved from responsibility, the tragedy cast a shadow
for a long time.

There were two aspects of the ill-fated Fanoe bids which
were to influence the future, one of them of much importance
to road safety generally apart from its effect on world land
speed record attempts. The apparently guilty 'beaded-edge'
and 'straight-sided' tyres (the latter were on the car when the
boy was killed) were put in the dock by the Dunlop Rubber
Company and from their investigations emerged the tyres of
tomorrow.

The other—human—factor which was to play such a large
part in the final Campbell story was that one of the three
mechanics who laboured so long on the Sunbeam before the
1923 Fanoe meeting was named Leo Villa. He would be there
when the final chapter was written some 44 years later.
Malcolm recorded his gratitude to Leo and to his other
principal supporter and mechanic, Harry Leech, and to the
Dunlop firm, in his book published in 1949, *Speed On Wheels*.

For the moment, the Campbell team worked on the car and
planned a new bid, one which would put the record firmly in
their grasp. A site for the attempt had to be found. Not
unnaturally, Southport and Saltburn were suggested, scenes
of many a speed trial. Someone put forward the idea of the
Pendine Sands in Carmarthenshire, and to the Pendine Sands
the team went. The fine stretch of sand here seemed to be ideal
for record-breaking, but on the day when Campbell made his
bid a strong wind was blowing and the sand was soft.

Conditions were, in Campbell's own words, 'vile', but,
possibly with pent-up frustration goading him on, he decided
to try for the record. He made four runs in each direction and
after them the average of his fastest two runs turned out to be
146.16 mph, just 0.15 mph better than Eldridge's figures. It
meant that at last Campbell was the world land speed record
holder but it wasn't good enough and he knew it. The record
was not likely to survive long against the other contenders now
entering the lists: Sunbeam were building a car for Henry
Segrave; Parry Thomas was hard at work at Brooklands; and

an Italian in Paris was building a car financed by an Egyptian prince and said to be capable of reaching 180 mph. Campbell had a slightly more 'down-to-earth' target but a real one nevertheless, the spur of being the first man in the world to reach 150 mph. He decided that he too would build a car capable of 180 mph but, failing to interest any established manufacturer, made up his mind to go it alone. Plans were put in hand for the new car, which was to be powered by a 450 horse-power Napier-Lion aero engine, but it soon became obvious to him that some of the other contenders would be in the field before the new machine was ready.

He made up his mind to have one more try with the Sunbeam. After all, the car had proved its worth and if capable of breaking the record in the gale conditions which had applied at Pendine on the previous bid, it should do better under more normal weather conditions. So, in July 1925, they were off to Pendine again.

The car still had the streamlined body and discs on the rear wheels but longer exhaust pipes had been fitted and the windscreen discarded. For once, Campbell said afterwards, everything went without a hitch. He put his foot flat on the floorboards and held it there and when the times were worked out he had averaged 150.87 mph, the first man to set the world record above 150. As has so often happened in other spheres of activity—the four-minute mile in latterday athletics is a good example—this achievement caught the imagination of the public.

The official Sunbeam candidate was swift to take up the challenge. Henry Segrave (Major H. O. D. Segrave to give him his full title then) had been engaged to drive the car and as the only British (American-born of an English father and an American mother, and domiciled in Ireland!) driver to win International Grand Prix races (the French and Spanish) in the post-World War One period the choice could hardly have been faulted. The car was another matter. Coatalen not surprisingly worked on the basis of his successful Grand Prix cars, and indeed the finished product was very similar to the big racing-cars of the period. Light and compact, it was powered by a

V12 engine of 3,976 cc, generally thought to be the result of two Grand Prix engines 'suitably mated' as one writer described it. But this comparatively small power plant relied on a super-charger for maximum performance and here Sunbeams ran into trouble.

The record bid was to be made on the seven-mile stretch of sand at Southport and Coatalen hoped that the car's lightness would enable it to reach maximum speed in the limited space available. Somewhere along the line someone hopefully changed the name of the car from *Ladybird* to *Tiger*. It would be wrong to say that the tiger burned bright but certainly there was enough illumination to snatch the record, rather uncertainly, from Malcolm Campbell's not-too-strong grasp.

Some accounts say that the supercharger split six times during the runs leading up to the successful record attempt. Others say that sand got into the casing and caused the trouble. Certainly Captain J. S. Irving, Chief Engineer of the Sunbeam Company, wanted to send the car back to Wolverhampton for two smaller superchargers to be fitted in place of the one big one. But time—and tide—did not permit. So Segrave went for the record.

He was given instructions not to run the engine any longer than necessary in view of the supercharger trouble, and through the haze which lingered over the sands watchers saw hot oil and water poured into the car to avoid the usual warming-up period. The first run went well, certainly well enough to break the record despite the fact that Segrave, mindful of his instruc-tions, did not let the car go all out.

The return run was a different story. The car was going great guns when it hit an undulation in the sand and took off, soaring through the air for a distance of some 60 feet. The revs went right up—not surprisingly with a driver who had suddenly found himself airborne—and that was the end of that particular supercharger. It naturally reduced Segrave's overall speed for the attempt and when the figures were worked out he was fractionally slower than Campbell over the measured mile. But his time over the kilometre was 152.33 mph and that was good enough to make him the new holder of the world land speed record. It also set the scene for the battle between Segrave and Campbell which was to dominate the story of the record for the next few years. Incidentally, the *Tiger* and the one similar car built were both still going strong long after the Second World War.

Segrave suggested to Coatalen that Sunbeam build a faster car, which they decided to do, but meanwhile another contender was raring to go. This was Parry Thomas, whose Leyland-Thomas cars were the talking point of Brooklands. Thomas, oil-stained genius in a Fair Isle pullover, hadn't the money to produce a land speed record special.

So he decided to adapt what he had and by using giant aero engines take the record by sheer power. Count Louis Zborowski had captured the imagination at Brooklands with his Higham Special in which he lapped at 117 mph. The Higham was powered by an absolute colossus of an engine—a V12 Liberty aeroplane motor of no less than 26,907 cc. Zborowski, as his father had before him, crashed in a race and was killed. Thomas bought the Higham Special, streamlined the front, lengthened the tail—and proceeded to lap Brooklands at around 126 mph. The car, he decided, was fast enough to have a crack at Segrave's record.

So in April 1926, Thomas and *Babs*, as the special had been christened, turned up at Pendine Sands where Campbell had previously broken the record. Calmly and without fuss, Parry Thomas decisively beat Segrave's record by no less than 16.97 mph, a figure which made both Campbell's and Segrave's efforts look puny. Nor was he content to let the matter rest there. The following day he went out again and upped the record to 171.02 mph. Honour satisfied, he retreated to his workshops at Brooklands to study ways and means of extracting yet more power from *Babs*.

Simultaneously, work was progressing on Campbell's new *Bluebird* and on Segrave's new Sunbeam. But Thomas, by pushing the record up by nearly 20 miles per hour, had stiffened the task for both contenders.

Campbell especially found it a hard blow. His new car had been designed for 180 mph and here was Parry Thomas setting a record only eight or nine miles short of this figure—and without apparent effort.

With the menace of Segrave's new car in the background—and *that* was being designed to travel at 200 mph—Campbell realized that he must move quickly and lose no time if he was to recapture the record before Segrave was ready or Thomas prepared to return.

The year 1927 promised to be a thrilling one as far as the world land speed record was concerned.

Chapter Five

Battle of the Titans

BY DINT OF GREAT EFFORT *Bluebird* was made ready to tackle the world land speed record at the beginning of 1927 and the team set forth for Pendine Sands. The car, on which most of the design work had been done by Amherst Villiers, was powered by a 450 horse-power 12-cylinder Napier-Lion aero engine. It had been three years in the building and almost met with disaster the moment it was pushed out on to the sands, sinking up to the axles in the soft surface and having to be hauled out by the many spectators, amongst them Parry Thomas, who had come for a first-hand view of one of his major rivals for the record.

Nor was that to be the end of a catalogue of woes and mishaps probably unique even in the long and troubled history of speed record attempts. Saved from sinking, *Bluebird* was found to be otherwise indisposed with gearbox and clutch troubles. Promptly Malcolm shipped her back to Povey Cross for the best 'medical' attention in his well-equipped workshops. Back to Pendine, more trouble, back to Povey Cross and then once more to Pendine. By this time it was February and the lorry used as a transporter had done more record-breaking or at least more travelling than *Bluebird*.

Sea-shells cut the tyres and on one run the car skidded into marker posts. The weather was bad and Campbell himself, as he afterwards admitted, had the feeling that ill-luck would be his permanent companion if he persisted in trying to gain and hold the record.

At last there was some improvement in the weather and *Bluebird* was wheeled out for another try. The first run went perfectly and the time over the measured distance was given as 179 mph. A similar run on the return trip would give Campbell the record comfortably. However, the jinx which pursued him had one more trick to play.

The run began without incident but as the car speeded towards its maximum it hit a bump. Campbell was jerked upwards, the wind tore at his goggles and he was half blinded by a shower of sand and water. He kept his foot hard down and with only one hand on the wheel (the other was trying to restore his vision) managed to hold a more-or-less straight course. Despite an obvious loss of speed, he felt sure that the record was his and he was right. The official figures were announced as 174.88 over the kilometre, 174.2 over the mile.

Three years of effort, of sweat, strain, hard work and great expenditure, had resulted in *Bluebird* capturing the record—but by less than four miles an hour. No one knew better than Campbell himself that he was unlikely to retain the title of the world's fastest driver for very long. In only a week or two, Segrave, with the Sunbeam Company's new contender, was aboard the *Berengaria* on his way to the United States and Thomas was en route to Pendine again, this time not to observe but to regain his title.

He had originally planned to be at Pendine just a few days after Campbell's successful bid but was laid low by an attack of influenza from which he was still not fully recovered by the beginning of March, although he decided he could brook no further delay. *Babs*, still further streamlined and with light fairings over the external driving chains, was transported to the sands on a hired, solid-tyred Scammell lorry. The young man in charge of transportation was named Paul Wyand and in later years was to make his mark in another fashion, first as a cameraman and then as News Editor of British Movietone News. Paul, a genial character and good friend, never forgot his early days in motor sport and was always happy to talk about Parry Thomas and Brooklands. He died in 1968, still the key man of Movietone News, still retaining his connection with motor sport as a member of the RAC Press Credentials Committee and, alas, regrettably young. He was only 61.

We digress. At Pendine, in March 1927, the weather was little improved over that 'enjoyed' by Campbell. The team waited. Thomas spent his time alternately on the beach, glaring at the sea as if he could mesmerize the weather into behaving, and in bed at his hotel trying to shake off the effects of his recent bout of flu.

On Thursday, March 3rd, it was decided to go ahead. *Babs* was driven down a slipway on to the sands and made two very fast runs. Eye-witnesses said the car was emitting a great deal of black smoke and there also seems to have been some query over the timing of the two runs. In any event, some slight adjustments were made to the car and Thomas set off again. With a tremendous roar the car swept over the measured mile and then came the most terrible disaster. One of the almost prehistoric driving chains broke, tore through the light aluminium fairing and flailed into the cockpit, almost beheading the unfortunate driver. A wheel came off, the car slid upside down for some distance, burst into flames and finally came to rest right side up and facing the direction from which it had started. Thomas's chief mechanic, Jock Pullen, risked his life and suffered burns in pulling his employer's body from the wreckage.

Exactly what did happen no one will ever know. The most feasible explanation is that proffered by Reid Railton who examined the wreckage carefully immediately after the accident and decided that a wheel had collapsed and a piece of spoke lodged between chain and chain-wheel had caused the chain to break.

The tragic story was blazoned over the front pages next day and when Thomas was buried at Byfleet, near the Brooklands which had been so much a part of his life, the tributes included many from men who also figured prominently in the story of the world land speed record, amongst them Sir Charles (later Lord) Wakefield, of Castrol fame; Reid Railton; John Cobb; Captain Malcolm Campbell; Kenelm Lee Guinness and Captain George Eyston.

Babs, every part smashed to discourage souvenir hunters, was buried in the sands of Pendine and Thomas's coat and driving helmet with her. (In 1969, *Babs* was disinterred and plans were made to restore the car.) *The Autocar*, as it was then before 'The' was dropped from the title, started a fund and Parry Thomas's memorial is a cot in the Great Ormond Street Children's Hospital, a tribute to a very brave and gallant man.

Whilst all this was happening, Segrave was on the high seas on his way to Daytona, Florida. The new Sunbeam was powered by two Matabele aero engines, one fore and one aft, giving it a cubic capacity of 44,880, more than twice the size of *Bluebird*, the record-holder. It was the tremendous potential of this giant car which made Segrave decide upon Daytona Beach for his attempt. It had been calculated that he would need a stretch of at least nine miles in which to start up, cover the measured mile and slow down again, and there was nowhere in Europe suitable for the purpose. At Daytona, however, scene of Marriott's steamer record in 1906, there was a stretch of almost 23 miles. So, despite the tremendous expense and negotiations which had to be launched to make sure that a record set in the States would be internationally recognized, Daytona it was.

Segrave had another problem also, the question of tyres. Were there any which would be safe at a speed of 200 mph? Dunlops came up with the answer but warned Segrave that they would guarantee the life of the tyres at only $3\frac{1}{2}$ minutes, just enough time to cover the measured distance and come to rest again: a frighteningly slender margin of safety. The news of how Parry Thomas met his death also prompted another check on the Sunbeam's driving chains, although armour-plate fairings had been fitted over them in contrast to the thin aluminium sheeting which Parry Thomas had used.

Other problems loomed up including trouble with the Customs; the car going 'missing' whilst being transported across America by rail; and some totally unnecessary alterations to the gear ratios (which probably reduced the performance of the car) owing to wrong timing information being given to the team after trial runs.

Yet on March 29th, 1927, Segrave smashed all previous records and became the first man to beat 200 mph. Not, however, without incident. He applied the brakes at the end of his first run and to his horror found that very little happened.

(above) Malcolm Campbell almost swamped by the press after breaking the world water speed record at Coniston in 1939. The dark-haired journalist on the left facing the camera is the doyen of motoring correspondents, Laurie Cade of the *Star*. (*Photo by Allied Newspapers, Manchester*)

(below) Donald Campbell's *Bluebird*— land version—on a demonstration run at Goodwood. (*Photo by Dunlop Rubber Co.*)

Donald's *Bluebird II* on the lakeside at Coniston before his first attempt on the water speed record in 1949, at attempt which narrowly ended in failure. *Bluebird* was ballasted with 20,000 table-tennis balls to give her buoyancy. (*Photo by Fox Photos*)

In fact the heat had been so tremendous that the aluminium brake shoes had melted. Segrave was faced with the choice of taking to the dunes, lined with 30,000 spectators; going into the Halifax River which lay directly ahead; or driving into the sea. With cool deliberation he chose the sea and went into it at about 60 mph sending up a great cloud of spray. The car slowed, swerved landwards and Segrave calmly drove ashore again. The mechanics fitted new brake-shoes and the Sunbeam made the return run. The wind was in Segrave's favour on this run and he was able to ease off in time to avoid any more hair-raising finishes despite a speed of more than 207 mph, the mean of the two runs being 203.79 mph, nearly 30 mph better than Campbell's record.

Meanwhile, back at Povey Cross, Malcolm Campbell had been far from idle. A new *Bluebird* was under construction and, as a result of wind tunnel tests, streamlined fairings were constructed in front of and behind the wheels and a tail-fin fitted to stabilize the car and help to keep it on a straight course. The most important matter, however, was to find a suitable power unit. Campbell and his helpers reasoned that if they could get a single engine developing more power than the Sunbeam's duo, they would have a more compact car and consequently stand a much better chance of breaking Segrave's record. Campbell's determination and powers of persuasion coupled with some helpful Air Ministry officials made such an engine available—a 940 horse-power Napier-Lion engine which had been developed for the British entries in the Schneider Trophy air race. This engine was still on the secret list. Work on *Bluebird* proceeded through 1927 and the hopes of the little team were raised when Britain won the Schneider Trophy at a speed of 281.49 mph, a true guide to the capabilities of the new power unit.

Thomas had gone but Campbell and Segrave were not left with the field to themselves. Presumably as a result of Segrave's electrifying runs and the fact that America was now within the international fold, a number of challengers emerged in the States. Two of these were ready to go almost simultaneously with Campbell and it is worth turning aside a moment to look at them.

D

One was a giant. Sponsored by a wealthy Philadelphia businessman, J. H. White, the White-Triplex was a monster and probably the ugliest machine ever to go in for the business of record-breaking. Little or no attention had been paid to streamlining to reduce wind resistance, and instead the car relied entirely on the brute force of no less than three giant Liberty aeroplane engines, one mounted in front of the driver and the other two side by side behind him. The engines had a total capacity nearly twice that of the Sunbeam which held the record and almost four times that of Campbell's new *Bluebird*.

But this was nothing compared to the way the White-Triplex dwarfed the other American challenger, Frank Lockhart's *Black Hawk* Stutz. White's car had almost 27 times the capacity of the Stutz.

At this time the world was Frank Lockhart's oyster. From the dirt-track speedways of the West, the laughing young Californian, even then dreaming of building a record-breaker, had gone to Indianapolis, Mecca of American drivers, to act as relief driver to seasoned campaigner Pete Kreis in the classic 500 Mile Race of 1926. In works of fiction, the star goes sick, gets drunk or breaks a leg and the young unknown seizes his chance of fame and glory. Well, it sometimes happens that way in real life too.

Kreis *was* taken ill and when the white-painted Miller No. 15 rolled up to the starting-grid, Lockhart was at the wheel. The stands were crowded with 140,000 spectators and from the PA system wafted the time-honoured pre-race song, 'Back Home In Indiana'. Then the heavens opened, the rain fell and the cars were wheeled back into their sheds. More than an hour later, the rain ceased and anxious officials pronounced the track fit for racing. The field included some of the great names of the 500 like Harry Hartz, Guyot, Earl Cooper, the 1925 winner Peter De Paolo and, perhaps surprisingly for those who think Brabham, Clark and Hill started the British invasion of 'Indy', two Englishmen, Douglas Hawkes and Ernest Eldridge. Lockhart took more than a passing glance at Eldridge for here was a man who had once held the world record Lockhart himself hoped to bid for one day. The race turned out a nip-and-tuck battle between the seasoned campaigner Harry Hartz and the rookie Lockhart, but when the rains came down again the race was halted after 400 miles. Lockhart was then in the lead and automatically declared the winner.

With $20,000 in his pocket and plenty of offers coming in, Lockhart retired to his workshop, plotting and planning his record-bid car. Like Parry Thomas he was much much more than a very fast racing driver and was indeed a brilliant engineer.

For the 1927 Indy, he prepared his own car and the magazine *Motor Age* commented:

'Perhaps the most thorough and workmanlike job of revising a rear-wheel drive type Miller car is seen in the Perfect Circle Miller driven by Frank Lockhart. Although classed as a young race chauffeur with a penchant for heavy footwear [Americanese for a driver who keeps his foot hard down on the floorboards], Lockhart would find no difficulty in qualifying as an experimental engineer. It is said that Lockhart's engine with his revisions develops in excess of 170 horse-power.'

For 109 laps the Perfect Circle Miller led the race, adding $10,900 to Lockhart's bankroll. Then a con-rod broke.

The next remarkable achievement of this remarkable young man was to take the Miller to the dry-lake beds of Muroc in his home State and there break international class records at a speed of 164 mph, an outstanding performance in a car of only 1500 cc, particularly when one bears in mind that Segrave's outright world record was only just over 200 mph.

So, in February 1928, *Bluebird*, the *Black Hawk* Stutz and the Triplex all put in an appearance at Daytona.

Campbell's first trial runs nearly brought disaster. The sands were not in especially good condition and a particularly obnoxious bump led to the car taking off and leaping some 30 feet through the air. The resulting four-point landing jarred every bone in Malcolm's body and damaged springs, shock absorbers and the underside of the car. This sort of thing had by now become all in the day's work to the Campbell team, who set to and repaired the damage. On February 19th, Campbell took the car out again.

Bluebird shot away over the measured mile but in the cockpit Malcolm was having to fight hard to keep her under control and again, just after clearing the measured distance, she hit a bump. Only Campbell's tight grip on the steering wheel saved him from being shot out. The car skidded and went into soft sand, Campbell still wrestling with the controls, and finally straightened out. Campbell turned round immediately and went back over the measured mile without stopping to change tyres as he should have done.

Afterwards, confessing that he thought his last moment had come on that first run, he said: 'I knew that if I stopped and got out of the car, I should never step into the machine again that day.'

This time fortune favoured the brave. Campbell was so exhausted that he had to be lifted almost bodily out of the car, but he perked up when the news came that he had beaten Segrave's record with a speed of 206.96 mph.

Next day, Lockhart and Ray Keech, a crack Indianapolis driver who had been engaged to handle the White-Triplex, both made trial runs, and the following day the *Black Hawk* came out again for a crack at the new figures.

The little white-painted car was said to have cost in the region of £30,000 which made it the most expensive contender up to that time. It was certainly very attractive, probably the best-looking car to try for the record apart from Segrave's *Golden Arrow* which was to come on the scene later, and with an engine of only 3,000 cc was one of the smallest cars to engage in a record bid.

Despite the bad conditions caused by wind and rain, Lockhart was soon travelling at around 200 mph. But the elements were not to be denied. A sudden gust of wind caught the car, which skidded and dived into the sea, bouncing from breaker to breaker before finally come to rest in a seething maelstrom of steam and whirling waves. Miraculously, both car and driver escaped serious hurt, although Lockhart was taken to hospital.

That left Keech still to make his bid and few gave much for his chance of beating Campbell's figures. Little thought appears to have gone into the design of the White-Triplex and hurried modifications had been necessary to fit a makeshift reverse gear, a means of reversing being essential under international regulations. Shades of our Thomas and our Eldridge long ago! The pessimists were not confounded. A water connection on the front engine weakened and burst, Keech being so severely scalded that he was taken to join Lockhart in hospital. For the moment, the four-cornered international contest ended, the field and the honours left to the British and the Americans licking their wounds.

But not for long. Keech made a speedy recovery from his burns and two months later the White-Triplex was prepared for another attack on the record. On the first run Keech clocked nearly 204 mph but on the return, when he estimated his speed at nearly 220 mph, something went wrong with the timing apparatus and he was asked to make a fresh attempt. It proved a hazardous journey. At one stage the car leapt 50 feet through the air and Keech sustained a burnt arm from engine backfire. Just the same—and confounding the critics— the car swept through to a new mark of 207.55 mph, robbing Britain of an honour which people had come to regard almost as a right, thanks to Parry Thomas, Campbell and Segrave.

Keech now decided he had had enough of record-breaking, at least in this particular car. It is generally believed that he told Mr. White what he could do with the White-Triplex! His judgement about the car's dangerous handling was vindicated later when Lee Bible tried to raise the record in it, crashed and lost his life. Ironically, Keech himself did not survive long. After winning the 'big one' at Indianapolis in 1929, he met with a fatal accident at a race meeting in Altoona.

For the moment, the record was safely in the custody of the United States and it looked like staying there. Lockhart too had recovered from his accident and intended to try again with the beautiful *Black Hawk*. His trials proved satisfactory, the car exceeding the double century with ease. Then, at speed, a tyre burst, the little 'dream' car skidded and overturned and the driver was thrown out, being killed instantly. One can but reflect on what the history of record-breaking might have been had Lockhart lived, remembering that his last officially timed run before the crash was 203.45 mph in a car of only 3,000 cc.

Segrave and Campbell were not wasting time whilst the Americans were trying again. Captain J. S. Irving had designed a new car for Henry, the *Golden Arrow* previously mentioned, and Campbell was not only redesigning *Bluebird* but was looking for pastures new in which to try to break the record. *Golden Arrow* was a thing of beauty and its streamlining left all previous contenders far behind. Irving had not been ashamed to borrow Campbell's idea of a Schneider Trophy engine and so the *Arrow* had the same power unit as *Bluebird*. The body was built to 'fit' Segrave by Thrupp & Maberly, better known for elegant town carriages, and in front of Segrave was a gun-sight so that he could, quite literally, 'aim' the car.

The ease with which the car regained the world record for Britain was almost anticlimax. Without ever being fully extended on a soaking wet beach, the Irving-designed beauty covered both runs over the measured mile at speeds of over 230 mph and smashed the record by some 24 miles an hour with an official speed of 231.44 mph.

Whilst Segrave was toying with the idea of trying to raise the record still more, Lee Bible took out the White-Triplex, worked up speed and was soon travelling at four miles a minute. A skid and the car drove crabwise into a newsreel cameraman. Car, cameraman and driver were smashed into oblivion. It was generally supposed at the time that Bible lifted his foot too quickly from the throttle, causing the overrun of the engines to act as a brake. The sudden braking effect threw the car into a skid from which Bible could not recover.

With American challenges so tragically ended, for the time being at any rate, Segrave returned home and was knighted for his achievement. The king sent him a message which read: 'On your arrival home I send you my hearty congratulations on your splendid achievement in winning for Great Britain the World's Speed Record for Motor Cars, and on your success in the International Speed Boat Trophy. George, R.I.'

The news reached Malcolm Campbell many miles across the ocean—in South Africa.

Chapter Six

Pastures New

AS THE WORLD RECORD crept and, in some cases, leapt upwards, so the Arpajons, Southports and Pendines faded from the scene, at least as far as fast cars and the men who drove them were concerned.

Malcolm Campbell, after some hair-raising experiences at Daytona, was sure that somewhere in the world there must be a better site for record attempts and he began a search, including an air trip to the Sahara, which took in many countries. Just when all possibilities seemed exhausted, a communication was received from South Africa suggesting a great dried-up lake bed, some four or five hundred miles from Cape Town, known as Verneuk Pan.

Campbell asked for detailed reports on the Pan and was excited by what he was told. The Pan was flat, there was no trouble from sea and tides and it was possible to mark out a straight stretch of at least 20 miles. There were some stones on the surface of the lake-bed but there was plenty of native labour available to deal with that problem. Some accounts say that he made a personal inspection of the site before making up his mind, but this seems unlikely in view of what eventually transpired, and those close to him say he ignored advice to see for himself before embarking on an expedition.

An expedition it turned out to be. Apart from *Bluebird*, the team, which included Malcolm's wife and their two children, Jean and Donald, had to transport spare parts, timing equipment, fuel, food and other stores through hundreds of miles of scrub and rough country. When finally all preparations were complete and they set out they were not unlike the pioneer Boer farmers trekking off in a wagon train.

No Eldorado awaited them at the end of the trek. The

stones which were to be easily swept away turned out to be ridges of pebbles, many of which when removed revealed outcrops of shale which could be shifted only by mechanical means. The plentiful native labour proved markedly reluctant to venture anywhere near the place and those who did speedily deserted in large numbers. To top it all, when *Bluebird* was started up there were soon signs of carburation trouble. No one had realized how the car might be affected by the fact that Verneuk Pan was some 2,000 feet above sea level.

Malcolm, as we have previously seen, was a man not readily discouraged. He sought help from the authorities in Cape Town and they suggested that a suitable surface could be prepared on the Pan by laying a mixture of mud. There was only one snag. For mud-making, water was required—and the nearest water-hole was five miles away! Undeterred, Malcolm asked for the work to begin. All of these headaches necessitated frequent journeys between the Pan and the Cape and Campbell undertook these in his own Gipsy Moth plane. On one of these trips he crash-landed and sustained quite severe injuries to his nose and mouth. After many stitches had been inserted in the wounds he resumed his journey in another plane—which promptly overturned on landing at the Cape. The injuries were reopened and Campbell was forced to the sidelines for several weeks.

Meanwhile, preparations at the Pan were going ahead steadily, so in spite of everything he was not too unhappy. He decided to celebrate his birthday—March 11th—in Cape Town and when he reached there he was handed a most unwelcome birthday present: Segrave had boosted the record to 231 mph. Any pleasure that Britain had regained the laurels was more than outweighed by the disastrous effect on his own plans. *Bluebird* had been designed for a maximum speed of about 230 mph, so the present attempt was doomed from the outset.

Campbell, however, was determined that he would not return home empty-handed. If there was no possibility of taking the record over the measured mile at least he could have a shot at the world five-mile record. And so he did, setting a mark of 211 mph which bettered the existing record by some 70 mph.

In the process, *Bluebird* also beat the five-kilometre record which had been set by Segrave during his Daytona bid. All in all, it was an excellent performance, but where motor-car speed records were concerned only one really counted, and Segrave held that at 231 mph.

There was still no shortage of contenders. The Egyptian *Djelmo* had finally been completed about a year previously but met an inglorious end on Pendine Sands, the car being a write-off although the Italian driver Foresti was thrown clear and miraculously unhurt.

Meanwhile, as Campbell reconsidered his position and wondered if, even with the financial help of that patron saint of record-breakers, Sir Charles (later Lord) Wakefield, it was worth while starting all over again and building a new car, yet another challenger appeared on the scene. This was a new Sunbeam, a powerful monster 31 feet long and with 4,000 horse-power engines which dwarfed even the American White-Triplex. It was to be handled by the British racing motorist, Kaye Don.

Despite the stable from which it came, the *Silver Bullet*, as it was known, turned out to be a colossal disappointment and at Daytona the most Kaye Don was able to manage was 186 mph. An attempt on the other side of the world in New Zealand fared a little better, 'Wizard' Smith in a Napier-Lion-engined special not unlike *Golden Arrow* clocking well over 200 mph but failing to get within reach of Segrave's record.

Campbell, of course, having thought the matter over had made the decision one would have expected—to rebuild *Bluebird* and have another go. The main modification was to substitute the latest Napier Schneider Trophy engine which was considerably more powerful than the old unit. Otherwise many parts of the original car were still retained.

New Zealand and South Africa were considered and discarded as venues for the attempt and finally it was to Daytona again that the team went. For once Fortune smiled kindly on Malcolm, and compared with his previous bids this one passed almost without incident. True, the spectators who had a close-up view of *Bluebird* at the end of one run never knew how lucky they were. It was only by frantic use of gears and brakes that Campbell managed to stop the car just 40 yards short of the crowd.

In almost every other respect things went well, and when Campbell's mechanics rushed to meet him after two completed runs it was with the joyful news that the record had been broken. His average time was 245.74 mph over the mile, more than 14 mph better than Segrave's figures, and 246.09 over the kilometre.

This time Campbell intended to hold the record if he could and had no intention of being caught napping by someone else as had occurred in the past. Reid Railton immediately began work on *Bluebird* with modifications designed to raise her performance still more. 'Wizard' Smith was said to be set on having another try, there were rumours that a further American challenge was in the offing, and besides, Campbell himself was now within reach of that magic 250 mph.

First, there were celebrations, official and otherwise, for his new record. Like Segrave before him, Malcolm stepped from the liner at Southampton to find that the accolade of knighthood was to be bestowed upon him, and cheering crowds met him everywhere.

The Americans could hardly wait to get him back and so with a modified car and an official invitation from the City of Daytona in his pocket he set sail again for the States. Once more the story is swiftly told. *Bluebird* averaged 253.97 mph for the two runs and Campbell had become the first driver to exceed 250 mph. Challengers or no challengers, he now had his vision firmly fixed on the next 'landmark'—300 mph. It was obvious that no minor modifications could make *Bluebird* go this fast in her present form, so once again Reid Railton got to work and the answer came in the form of a Rolls-Royce racing aeroplane engine which was fantastically light for the tremendous power it generated.

The car had to be lengthened and strengthened but at last all was ready and in February 1932 Malcolm Campbell was given a brass-band welcome back to Daytona. Bad weather and the condition of the beach delayed any question of an attempt for a couple of weeks and Malcolm, who had been rather unwell with a touch of influenza, was glad of the breathing space.

His first trial run was not a happy one. Conditions were far from ideal but more serious was the fact that he strained his left arm in forcing the gear-lever into top.

In spite of this he determined to press on. Heavy mist wafted in from the sea as he essayed the first run, but this did not deter some 50,000 spectators from coming along to see the drama. *Bluebird* sped southwards at nearly 274 mph and made the return journey around 270, thus giving a new record of 272.46 mph, a major step forward towards the 300 mark. The real drama was not observed by the spectators since only Leo Villa and his other faithful henchmen knew what pain Campbell was in from his left arm, which had to be massaged at the end of the first run in order to enable him to complete the second.

He was exhausted afterwards and was medically advised against further attempts until the arm improved. In any event the weather continued bad and finally the decision was taken to return home, where he received another hero's welcome.

Once again modifications to *Bluebird* began. This time there needed to be no serious rethinking about the engine since the Rolls-Royce unit still harboured untapped power. But Malcolm had realized during his recent successful runs that a great deal of that power was being lost through wheelspin. Although he was being officially timed at around 270 mph, the rev counter in fact indicated a speed nearer 330 mph. If a means could be found of harnessing that additional 50 or 60 mph, the 300 mph mark could be comfortably surpassed.

A means was found. Twin rear wheels were fitted, and a rear axle of new design, but complete success for these modifications was to be denied by the conditions at Daytona, where Campbell arrived, accompanied by Mrs. Campbell and Jean, in January 1935.

It was on this attempt that something was done which was afterwards to become standard practice. At Verneuk Pan, a white line had been painted down the centre of the course and Malcolm had found it a great help in keeping the car straight.

He mentioned this to the Daytona authorities, and a line two feet wide was painted in lampblack and oil.

After the first test run, a fortnight elapsed before it was decided that conditions, whilst not very good, were favourable enough for a serious bid to be made. It looked good at the start but then exhaust fumes and scorching heat forced their way into the cockpit and Campbell had to slow down. At the end of the run it was found that wind was lifting the bonnet, diverting flames and fumes into the car. Campbell made the return run but again the same thing happened and he was forced to slow down.

Mechanics worked hard on the car all night, and next day Campbell went out again. This time he did a very fast run but was nearly shot out of the cockpit because the bumps were so bad. He felt that to risk a return journey might cause serious damage to *Bluebird* and so decided to wait for another day and more favourable conditions. Two days later everything seemed satisfactory but just as the car was ready to start a high wind got up and again the attempt had to be abandoned.

Finally, on March 7th, a serious bid was possible although winds and mist lingered on. Against the wind, *Bluebird* slightly improved on the record, a cheerful note of optimism for the return journey. On the way back, however, the car hit an enormous bump just as it shot through the opening of the pier towards the measured mile. It was nearly the end of Campbell, the car taking off and coming down again with a tremendous crash. He had a desperate fight to keep it under control and went down the measured mile swaying from side to side at a tremendous pace. When he came safely to rest the world land speed record had been increased to 276.81 mph. Afterwards the distance of that leap through the air was measured and found to be more than 30 feet.

Positive that *Bluebird* was capable of greater things if only beach conditions improved, the Campbell team stayed on at Daytona for a total of eight weeks, giving up only when the beach deteriorated still more. It was obvious that if 300 mph was to be attained, a more suitable course than Daytona had to be found.

Found it was. In the heart of Mormon country, an American driver Ab Jenkins, who with his *Mormon Meteor* was to set record after record through the years, had successfully collected a number of long-distance marks on the salt flats at Bonneville, Utah. A gigantic lake-bed of some 500 square miles. the surface is under water in the winter when the rains come but in summer the water evaporates leaving a layer of hard salt. Although at a glance the surface appears smooth, the salt in fact hardens in ridges which have to be scraped off to give a surface suitable for record-breaking.

So to Utah they went to a sight difficult to imagine. Under glaring sunshine in a temperature over 100°F, the flats stretched out like some vast snowfield, a glittering white expanse which flung back the sun's rays and made dark glasses essential. The air was so clear that the Rocky Mountains fifty miles distant looked only a matter of hundreds of yards away.

The team made its headquarters at the little hamlet of Wendover some six miles from the course. Over the next decades, Wendover was to be the base for many history-making runs.

By September 1st, both course and car were ready and Campbell went out for a trial run. He was delighted with the results. The car ran well and there was no trouble with bumps on the surface as there had been at Daytona. True, salt covered the car like snow-flakes and caused trouble by packing hard between the wheels and the fairings, but this was soon remedied by cutting away part of the fairings.

If Campbell thought that all would go smoothly this time he should have known better. It was arranged that an attempt should be made early next morning, thus avoiding the worst of the heat. A 6 a.m. start was agreed upon but a spectator motorist had other ideas. He drove his car across the timing wires and broke them, causing an hour's delay before all was ready again.

Finally, *Bluebird* snarled away, building up speed towards the measured mile. Just before reaching it, Campbell pushed the lever, closing the radiator shutter and so reducing wind resistance. All hell broke loose. A film of oil spread over the windscreen, obscuring his vision, and exhaust fumes rushed into the cockpit. Desperately peering ahead, he kept his foot down and looked anxiously for the markers at the end of the mile which would be the sign that he could ease up. With relief he spotted them and began to slow down but his troubles were not yet over. A front tyre burst and caught fire, Campbell nearly losing control. The run ended with him breaking heavily and leaping out of the car to attack the burning tyre with a fire extinguisher.

Frantically work began to prepare the car for the return journey. Meanwhile a motor-cyclist arrive with the news that the first run had been timed at 304 mph. An hour was then allowed between runs and only fifteen minutes remained when the car was at last ready. Then came the message that the timing wires had again been broken and Campbell was forced to sit impatiently in his car in the full glare of the sun as the precious minutes ticked away.

With five minutes only remaining, the 'All Clear' was given and Campbell roared away, firmly deciding to avoid closing the radiator shutter even if it slowed him down a little. The run was incident-free and Campbell was sure that he had gone fast enough to push the record over 300 mph. Then the time-keepers telephoned through: 299.9 mph. He had missed the magic mark by one tenth of a mile per hour. The disappointment of the whole team can be imagined.

The car was taken back to Wendover and mechanics began to beat out a cockpit cover which it was thought could increase the speed by 10 to 15 mph. Campbell, heart set on that 300 figure, was to have another go next morning.

Then came another message from the American Automobile Association timekeepers. There had been a mistake. Campbell's speed for the return journey had been 298.01 mph giving a mean speed of 301.13. They had done it after all. Malcolm was a bit dubious about this and told the officials that he thought he ought to go out again next day anyway and make sure of the record, but on being given categorical assurance that the 301.13 figure was accurate and would stand as official, he decided no useful purpose would be served.

His ambition achieved (although, as he afterwards said, much of the pleasure taken off by the blundering of the time-keepers), Malcolm decided that he would rest on his laurels as far as the land speed record was concerned. He had left an indelible mark on its history, having broken it no less than nine times, and had been personally responsible for adding the last 70 miles an hour to it.

From now on his record-breaking was to be of a different nature.

Chapter Seven

Record-breaking on Water

THE WORLD LAND SPEED RECORD had been a major part of Malcolm Campbell's life for a decade or more but it had not monopolized it to the exclusion of all else. He had continued racing both at Brooklands and on road circuits and had been one of the few British drivers to distinguish himself internationally.

In 1926, in the first ever British Grand Prix at Brooklands, he had finished second to Wagner in a Delage, with Benoist, Wagner's team-mate, in third place. In 1927 and again in 1928 he won the Brooklands 200 Mile Race, and in the former year won the National Trophy at Boulogne.

Two of Britain's classic races, the Tourist Trophy and the short-lived Irish Grand Prix, were not happy hunting grounds for him, and his best effort in these was a class win in the 1930 T.T. He hit the headlines, however, in the 1928 T.T., when his Bugatti caught fire and pictures of the conflagration with Malcolm vainly endeavouring to stem the flames were published all over the world.

The car was apparently not insured and its loss cost Malcolm more than a thousand pounds. When the flames died down souvenir-hunters descended like a flock of hungry vultures and picked the carcass clean!

In his ordinary race activities as distinct from his record-breaking attempts Campbell stayed faithful to the colour blue. So did his contemporary, Viscount Curzon (later Earl Howe), who eventually became Chairman of the RAC Competitions Committee. Earl Howe's liking for blue even extended to a blue umbrella which—long after his active racing career had finished—could be seen at Silverstone's Woodcote corner sheltering its owner from rain or sun.

The year 1930 (he missed the 1929 race) was not a much happier year for Malcolm as far as the T.T. was concerned—'handicapped out of the race' was how one observer put it. Just the same he finished 10th in a Mercedes (with Howe in a similar car 18th). But Alfa Romeo scored a convincing 1–2–3 win with that great trio of drivers, Nuvolari, Campari and Varzi.

At Brooklands, however, Campbell continued to be one of the dominating drivers and his successes were many. It was ironic that when in 1946 shareholders of the Weybridge circuit voted to sell out for £330,000 to the Vickers aircraft company —a decision which meant the end of Brooklands as a motor-racing venue—Campbell was one of the directors reported to be in full agreement. It was doubly ironical that one of the greatest opponents of the decision was Campbell's 'blue' colleague, Earl Howe. With the wisdom of hindsight, many people have criticized Campbell and the part he played in the demise of Britain's only permanent motor-racing track. It seems hard to believe that a man who had enjoyed such success at Brooklands would cheerfully preside at the funeral rites. It seems even harder to believe when one reads a fiction effort from Campbell, *Thunder Ahead*, which breathes a love for racing and a genuine affection for Brooklands in almost every line. But there it is—Brooklands died and one of its greatest drivers did not prevent the coffin being slid into the grave.

After 1930 Malcolm spent less and less time racing. His successes might have been more had not the land speed record played so large a part in his life and had there been British-manufactured cars capable of winning the great races. It was a source of mild regret to Malcolm that he was forced to drive foreign cars like Bugatti and Delage in order to stand a chance of winning. His contemporary 'Tim' Birkin spoke bitterly of the criticisms he, Campbell and Howe endured because they preferred to drive 'foreign' rather than not drive at all. 'Sir Malcolm Campbell has been attacked as if he had actually changed his name to Campbelline', said Birkin.

Motor-racing and record-breaking aside, Campbell was a man of many parts and fierce, if often fleeting, enthusiasms, amongst them golf, photography, collecting china and breeding dogs. One interest which never left him was the search for buried treasure. In this he did not content himself with merely studying the subject but went on several abortive expeditions.

The first of them, to the Salvage Islands in 1924, was a spur-of-the-moment effort and it was not until he returned home that he found that the silver he was seeking had been dug up by someone about a hundred years previously! A rather more serious expedition—to Cocos Island—was undertaken two years later in company with brother racing motorist and record-breaker Kenelm Lee Guinness, who had in his possession charts which supposedly led to buried pirate treasure, but in fact did not do so. It takes a great deal of cold water, however, to dampen the enthusiasm of your confirmed treasure-hunter and in 1934 he was at it again, this time an aerial expedition to find a gold reef off the coast of Africa.

It was too much to expect that his hobbies and enthusiasms, his work as motoring editor of the *Daily Mail* and motoring correspondent of *The Field*, and a brief foray into politics as an unsuccessful Conservative candidate at Deptford, would keep Malcolm away from the world of speed once he had announced his intention of withdrawing from the land speed record contest. There were still records to be broken and honours to be brought to Britain in another sphere of ultimate speed—the water.

Britain's racing drivers seem always to have had an affinity with the water, perhaps because of our 'island home', beginning with the great pioneer and winner of the 1902 Gordon Bennett race, S. F. Edge, who, after the 1903 race in the series, went to Cork and in a Napier-powered craft won the first Harmsworth Trophy Race for motor-boats.

The Briton who had played the most prominent part in the story of the water speed record was Malcolm Campbell's contemporary and fellow land speed record-breaker, Sir Henry Segrave, whose triumphs were achieved despite the handicap of silver plates in his left foot, a legacy of being shot down as an RFC pilot in 1916.

After *Golden Arrow*'s success on land, Segrave won the International Motor Boat Championship by beating the record-holder Gar Wood's *Miss America V* in the appropriately named *Miss England*. He followed up by winning the German Championship and later in the same year (1929) was timed unofficially on the Thames at 89 mph.

Next came the European Championships at Venice and here *Miss England* was up against the strongest opposition yet. Gar Wood brought over two boats, *Miss America V* and *Miss America VII*. The latter, 2,600 horse-power and twin-engined, had held the world water speed record since 1928 at a speed of 92.86 mph. The championship was decided by each competitor making six runs over a measured nautical mile and Segrave proved comfortably the fastest, his winning speed of 92.52 being very close to Wood's world record. Winning the Coppa Volpi which followed, Segrave was unofficially timed at a speed greater than the world record and it was obvious that a boat of similar design to *Miss England* but with more power could take the world title comfortably.

Backed by Sir Charles Wakefield, Segrave built *Miss England II*, powered with twin Rolls-Royce engines, to break the record and to wrest the Harmsworth Cup once won by Edge from the grasp of Gar Wood. The attempt was made at Lake Windermere on Friday, June 13th, 1930. The first two runs passed without incident but on the third *Miss England* capsized and sank. Segrave died shortly after being taken from the water. One of the engineers riding with him had been killed instantly, the other miraculously surviving.

But the record had been broken. The official mean time for the first two runs was 98.76 mph although unofficial timing for the third and fatal run was 119.8 mph.

Britain was not to hold the record for long, however, and soon the title was back in the United States. Then Kaye Don came on the scene with more success than he had enjoyed on land and, driving *Miss England III*, lifted the record to over 100 mph. For a time the record was a shuttlecock between *Miss England III* and a succession of *Miss Americas* produced by the indefatigable Gar Wood. When the smoke of battle finally cleared, the American was in possession of the field. The official record stood to *Miss America X* at a speed of 124.8.

At this point Malcolm Campbell decided to take a hand. So Bluebird *I*, a wooden-hulled boat powered by the engine from Campbell's land record holder, came into being and, after trials on Loch Lomond in 1937, was taken to Lake Maggiore for an attempt on Gar Wood's record.

On September 1st, the boat was taken out and the record pushed up to 128.3 mph, but Malcolm felt that this was not a good enough improvement to hold off another challenge from the American, so next day he went out again. This effort raised his own record another fraction to 129.5 mph. No American counter-attack was immediately forthcoming so in 1938 on Lake Hallwill Campbell had another try and edged the figure up to nearly 131 mph.

It was still not good enough to hold off any determined challenge and work was put in hand on *Bluebird II*. The power plant remained the same but the boat itself was of revolutionary design and evolved by Reid Railton who had designed the later *Bluebird* land speed record cars.

In August 1939, *Bluebird II* was taken out on Coniston Water and the water speed record was raised to 141.74 mph. Within a fortnight the world was at war and Malcolm Campbell was back in the army.

Six long years later, Campbell was back in 'Civvy Street' and excited by the possibilities of using jet engines in motor-boats. His world water speed record remained intact since most people in Britain and the United States, not to mention the rest of the world, had had other things on their minds during the past few years. Now Malcolm's ambition was to raise that record to 200 mph, using jet engines in *Bluebird*, and so put it beyond reach of the Americans who, it was rumoured, were hard at work on some new challengers.

The hull of *Bluebird II* was reconstructed at Portsmouth and De Havillands loaned, by permission of the Air Ministry, a 4,000 horse-power Goblin jet engine. The boat was completed during the summer of 1947 and sent up to Coniston Water where the new bid was to be made.

It was a short-lived attempt. At 100 mph, the boat swerved off course and this happened time and again until the decision was taken to sent it back to Portsmouth. Here it was decided to fit a fin underwater, and after further trials conducted in Poole Harbour by Malcolm himself the team again went to Coniston in August 1948.

Bad water conditions delayed the attempt and when *Bluebird III* was taken out at last Campbell reached only 120 mph before difficulties appeared in the handling. No one will ever know just what was wrong on this last and least successful of all Malcolm Campbell's record attempts. He was 62 years of age and already a sick man. By the following year he was dead. Whatever the snags which attended his last efforts to push the water speed record still higher, it seems certain that the veteran Malcolm Campbell, not surprisingly, had lost some of that tremendous drive and vitality which had enabled him to triumph over disasters in the past.

It was sad that such a magnificent career had to end on a note of anticlimax. Campbell had already suffered a slight stroke and been ordered to take things quietly by his doctor. Then his sight began failing and he had to undergo operations before the 1947 attempts. Nevertheless, enough remained of that dynamic urge to keep him working almost until the end, and only weeks before his death he demonstrated a fluid transmission unit he had invented to experts from the Admiralty.

Whatever his faults—and he had many critics—Malcolm Campbell had kept Britain's prestige high. Between the two wars Campbell, Segrave, Parry Thomas, Kaye Don and others had ensured that Britain was 'the one to beat' where the world land and water speed records were concerned, and of these it is arguable that Sir Malcolm Campbell, nine times land speed record holder and four times water speed record holder, was the greatest.

Knighted by his king, he was also honoured by his fellows and became the first man ever to be twice awarded the Segrave Trophy, given in memory of Sir Henry for 'the British subject who accomplishes the most outstanding demonstration of the possibilities of transport by land, air or water'.

Campbell was awarded it in 1933 for his land speed record at Daytona and again in 1939 for his water speed record at Coniston. No one else would be awarded the Segrave Trophy twice or more until long after the Second World War.

The name of that man would be Donald Campbell.

Chapter Eight

Picking up the Torch

THE WAR HAD BROUGHT some disappointment to Donald Campbell, the RAF deciding that piloting a plane and a history of rheumatic fever were not a compatible combination. One can only guess at what went through his mind at that time although the present author, who had a similar experience, has a good idea. Anyway, there was nothing to be done about it and Donald went on earning a living as an engineer.

At what period he seriously contemplated assuming his father's mantle as a record-breaker is also a matter of conjecture. It may well be that the thought was partly formed in those now distant days when his father had admonished him for taking his pedal-car to pieces. But we have the word of Leo Villa, who as chief mechanic served the Campbells for 45 years, that within a few weeks of Malcolm's death Donald had summoned him to say that he intended to 'start where the old Dad left off'.

It was a hard task which Donald Campbell set himself back in 1949. Not least of the handicaps was the ghost of a dead father. The pages of sporting, political and industrial history are spotted with the names of sons of famous fathers who tried desperately to live up to the achievements of their parents. Some succeeded, many more did not. Not a few did remarkably well on their own account but still found themselves dwarfed by the long shadow cast by their parent.

Another of the handicaps that Donald faced was the grim truth that he had no experience whatsoever in racing either cars or boats. His father had started his record-breaking career after an apprenticeship in racing both motor-cycles and cars, and record-breaking on land had been a comparatively simple extension of the sprints and hill-climbs in which he had proved himself a successful competitor.

The world of record-breaking and racing was unknown to Donald when he made his 'declaration of intent' to Leo Villa that day in 1949. He had only his knowledge of his father, the loyal support and vast 'know-how' of Villa and his own determination on the credit side of the ledger. They were to be enough, although the first steps were to be faltering ones.

It was decided to attempt the world water speed record which, of course, still stood to Sir Malcolm after his fine performance in 1939. But with Malcolm's ill-fated post-war attempts and Donald's lack of experience very much in mind, Leo Villa suggested that it would be best to replace the jet engine in *Bluebird* with a piston engine similar to the one used in 1939. It was not as simple as it sounds since various 'bits and pieces' had been sold and Donald had to sacrifice the 1935 *Bluebird* car in the absence of sufficient ready cash to buy everything needed.

Finally all was ready, and in August 1949 the *Bluebird* outfit returned to Coniston Water. Then began the familiar pattern which accompanies most record attempts. Donald handled the boat well from the outset but the pressure was on, the press of the world was waiting to hail or to jeer, and the weather, so important for success, began to play its usual tricks. More than three weeks went by before a serious bid was possible and then, with the boat flat out, Donald was blinded by a jet of oil shooting into the cockpit and had to ease off. Despite this he was greeted with the good news that the record had been broken. There seemed no doubt about it and newspapers and radio broadcast the story to the world. Then came anticlimax. There had been a mistake in the time-keeping and Sir Malcolm's figures of 141.74 mph were still intact. The disappointment of that moment would have been enough to deter a lesser man.

Not Donald, however. If anything he was more determined than ever. Modifications were carried out on the boat and less than a year after the abortive attempt, in June 1950, Coniston awoke once more to the roar of engines across the lake.

It seems fantastic now but this time two shattering disappointments were in store. First of all, on a trial run, the engine 'blew up'. Then, whilst a replacement engine was being fitted, the most staggering news of all came across the Atlantic. The water speed record had been in the Campbell family so long that no one had given a thought to other possible challengers for the title. Now the ticker-tapes flashed the news that an American, Stanley Sayers, had not only broken Sir Malcolm's record but had raised the figure to a devastating 160.32 mph. It was like a blow in the kidneys to the Campbell team who returned south to, in effect, start all over again.

There was no suggestion of giving up and work on the boat began immediately with the help of some expert advisers. Yet no one could deny that a shot in the arm was needed after the heartbreaks of those two ill-fated attempts at Coniston. It came in a somewhat unexpected fashion with an invitation from the Italians to compete in the 1951 Oltranza Cup race on Lake Garda. There was a special significance to the invitation since the cup had been originally donated in memory of Sir Henry Segrave and several British drivers had subsequently tried to win it.

And win it Donald Campbell did, with Leo Villa, on his own admission, swearing and praying alternately as he hung on for dear life in the observer's seat. Lapping at nearly 100 mph, *Bluebird* gained a well-deserved if frightening victory which was just the tonic Donald and his ménage needed.

Yet if any of them thought that the Italian success was a good omen they were to be sadly disillusioned. The Lake Garda race was in June and immediately afterwards *Bluebird* was shipped to Lake Coniston. Work went on in the light of the Italian experience but not all went well and the summer days slipped away with the boat not ready, the weather not right, the water too choppy, the engine running 'rough'. It was October, with the chilly fingers of winter wraith-like on the northern landscape, before the boat seemed to be nearing the right condition of perfection to make a serious attempt feasible. Early one morning, with the lake surface as smooth as a looking-glass, Campbell and Villa went out for a trial run. They were travelling at an estimated 170 mph when the boat spun into the air, threshed the water wildly like a harpooned whale in its death throes and began to sink. Campbell and Villa were fished out but *Bluebird* sank in 25 feet of water whilst being towed to shore.

When she was raised, the reason for the disaster became clear. A submerged railway sleeper had torn a great hole in her bottom. The boat was a wreck and it was obvious that nothing could be done to make her water-worthy again. To Donald Campbell, to Leo Villa, to their helpers, it looked like the end of an odyssey and yet another son had failed to emulate the deeds of a famous father. The urge was still there, the financial resources necessary to sustain world record-breaking were not. Donald Campbell returned to his engineering business and Villa went with him. The Campbell story could well have ended there and Donald today might be a flourishing Surrey business-man, wrestling with nothing more frightening than income tax and S.E.T. returns. Indeed, for a time it looked as this might be the outcome as he turned to the business of making a living in light industry.

Meanwhile, other record-breakers had not been idle. In particular, John Cobb, 'the fastest man on earth', had justly been in the limelight after becoming the first to achieve the magic 400 mph on land.

Cobb, a burly City business-man, had captured the world record on the eve of the outbreak of World War Two, tooling his giant Railton over the Bonneville Salt Flats at an average speed of 369.70 mph. After war service with the RAF and the Air Transport Auxiliary, John had returned to 'Civvy Street' chagrined to find that Brooklands, where he had driven so often and so successfully, had been sold. His biographer, Bentley 'boy' Sammy Davis, says that Cobb was most bitter about this and laid the blame largely at the door of Malcolm Campbell. However, he did not waste much time in mourning and was soon on his way to the States in a bid to be the first man to travel at 400 mph. On September 15th, 1947, he did so, clocking 403.135 mph in one direction and averaging 394.196 for a new land speed record, nearly 25 miles an hour faster than his previous figure. He was just in time. Next day the rains came and the Salt Flats were flooded.

He was awarded the Segrave Trophy but, unlike Segrave and Malcolm Campbell before him, received no knighthood. Strange in the light of the precedents which had been set, even more strange in view of the many knighthoods for sporting achievement and endeavour which were to come a decade or two later.

Cobb turned, as Segrave and Campbell had turned, to the world water speed record. Vospers built a specially designed jet-powered boat for him, *Crusader*, and Loch Ness was chosen for the attempt. In the perfection of a September day in Scotland—and is there anything better?—Cobb and *Crusader* set off. The boat appeared to be travelling perfectly, the speed gradually increasing until it was moving at record-breaking velocity. Then the stern went down into the water, there was a great explosion and a cloud of steam and spray. The hoodoo which seems to hang over water speed record-breaking had caught up with Cobb. The date was September 29th, 1952.

Cobb's land speed record looked like standing for some time, but now that he was gone and Donald Campbell had 'retired' from the record-breaking scene it appeared that the American grip on the water speed record would not be weakened. Donald was restless, however, under his self-imposed 'ban' and before a year had expired had called in Villa and the designer brothers, the Norrises, and launched plans for a new boat. His first marriage had broken up and he had married again, this time a girl from New Zealand. In every sense, a new chapter had been opened.

The new boat was to have a metal hull and be jet-propelled, and some idea of the planning and hard work which must go into such a project can be gained from the fact that three years were to elapse before in 1955 the second *Bluebird* was to take to the water. In the meantime the target had moved dramatically upwards and the American holder, Stanley Sayers, pushed the record up to 178 mph. That meant that unless the new *Bluebird* could clock in the region of 200 mph it would all be wasted effort. A water speed of 200 mph was just as significant a milestone as 400 mph had been on land. No man had achieved it unless one counts Cobb and the Italian Mario Verga, both of whom were thought to have passed the mark during their last tragic runs.

By July 1955 all was ready. This time another expanse of water in the Lake District, Ullswater, had been chosen for the attempt, giving a 'run-up' of some three and a half miles before the boat entered the measured stretch. The morning of July 23rd, although overcast, was dry and windless and the boat was taken out. Given a report on the conditions, Donald decided that this was it.

The cockpit cover closed over him, the engines started up and *Bluebird* began building up speed. By the time he hit the measured distance, the boat was travelling at a terrific rate but looked steady as a rock. Campbell turned and made the return run and knew, even before the official timekeeper appeared on the jetty, that he had triumphed at last.

When the figures were given, they were truly magnificent. The record had come back to Great Britain with a speed of 202.32 mph and Campbell had made his own little niche in history as the first man to travel at over 200 mph on water.

There was a farcical anticlimax when he accepted an invitation to go to the United States and *Bluebird* sank on Lake Mead, swamped by the wash of sightseeing boats which crowded around her, but a month later Donald emphasized that the record had been no fluke by pushing his own figure up to a staggering 216.25 mph. Leo Villa has said: 'We were turning our backs on six years of frustration and failure, and a great wave of happiness broke over us.'

Chapter Nine

Taste of Bitterness

LIKE SWIMMING ON A WINTER MORN, once you've broken the ice there is nothing to it—much. Having claimed the world water speed record at long last, Donald Campbell was to break it again and again. After his double success in 1955, he succeeded year by year in pushing the figure higher. England was the background to each of these bids as in 1956 he raised the mark to nearly 226 mph; in 1957 to 239 mph; in 1958 to almost 249 mph; and in 1959 to more than 260 mph. In the process he became the more or less permanent possessor of the Royal Motor Yacht Club's Andre Trophy.

Few sporting trophies have a more interesting history. Originally the Britannia Trophy, it was presented by the Prince of Wales, later to become King Edward VII, in 1870 for open competition amongst schooners. Then for years it completely disappeared before being unearthed in an old Kentish silvermaker's in 1937.

The man who found the cup was Mr. T. B. Andre, then a committee member of the Royal Motor Yacht Club, who had the trophy renovated and then presented it to the club. It was decided that it should be awarded annually to the holder of the world water speed record and the first recipient was, not surprisingly, Sir Malcolm Campbell for his 141.74 mph in *Bluebird* on Lake Maggiore, Italy. The cup went to America in 1950 when Stanley Sayers recorded 178.497 mph but Donald Campbell and *Bluebird* won it back for Britain on July 23rd, 1955, with that 202.32 mph record on Ullswater.

The trophy was to remain Campbell's for the rest of his life, the culmination being at the Royal Motor Yacht Club's Diamond Jubilee Dinner at the London Hilton on November 18th, 1965, when he once again received it in recognition of his

276.33 mph record run on Lake Dumbleyung, Australia, on
the last day of 1964. But that was still in the future in late
summer, 1955, as Donald and his faithful henchman Leo Villa,
happy in the possession of the water speed record, contemplated
the future and asked themselves, 'Where do we go from here?'

On the way ahead lay triumphs and tragedies, bitterness
and disappointment and happiness too. Donald's marriage to
the New Zealand girl, Dorothy, had broken up and he was
vowing 'never again'. But in the course of time Donald was to
see an attractive Belgian girl, Tonia Bern, starring in cabaret
at London's Savoy Hotel and, in typical dynamic Campbell
fashion, meet, woo and marry her in the space of a few weeks.
Tonia was to be with him the rest of the way, through the
disasters and the victories, until, at the end, she stood a lonely
and silent figure on the shores of the waters which had claimed
her husband.

It was to be expected that Donald would not be content
with holding the world water speed record, and so it proved.
The land speed record was still held by John Cobb and Donald
determined that a new *Bluebird* would succeed to the title.
First came the search for sponsors and then designing, building
and preparing for the attempt. It all took time, time in which
the name of Campbell stayed in the public eye with repeatedly
successful bids to increase his own water speed record.

By 1960, the new *Bluebird* car was ready. Its destination was
the salt flats of Utah, where *Bluebird* arrived at the village of
Wendover on August 28th, to be garaged in a US Air Force
hangar which had once sheltered World War Two planes used
for training the crews who were to drop the atomic bomb on
Japan. It had been 25 years since Sir Malcolm Campbell had
used the same base in his successful bid to post a record of
300 mph. He had been accompanied then by Donald, age 14.

Not much was the same. The *Bluebird* team was probably
the largest ever: engineers and technicians, representatives of
manufacturers and backers, the total contingent numbering
almost 100 if one included pressmen. Apart from the car, there
was 35 tons of equipment, all of it transported 6,000 miles from
Britain. Support vehicles included two BP refuelling vehicles

and some specially equipped Landrovers. But perhaps the most interesting items were 80 huge tyres for *Bluebird*, the largest ever made for a land vehicle. Their diameter was no less than 52 inches. Nor did the Campbell outfit have Wendover to themselves. Three American teams were also on the spot to have a crack at Cobb's record.

Something else had altered from 1935, something with more ominous portents. Leo Villa said the salt flats themselves had altered since he was there with Sir Malcolm. Then they had been hard and white, now they were grey and mushy. In the light of subsequent events, Leo's comment took on special significance. Moreover, there had been a tragedy earlier in the summer when American Athol Graham had been killed in attempting to break the record.

Forebodings disappeared in the hustle and bustle of preparation. Certainly, if the thought which had gone into the advance preparations could be maintained, there seemed little need to worry. The equipment was plentiful and of the finest, the operational team included some of the most experienced and knowledgeable men in motoring, amongst them racing driver and journalist Tommy Wisdom as operational adviser; Peter Carr, as project director; designer Ken Norris; and, of course, Chief Engineer Leo Villa.

The car was wheeled out for the first time on September 5th, attracting tremendous interest both from press and public with people flocking out from Salt Lake City to see the car they had heard so much about. Donald undertook some preliminary trials and, by and large, expressed himself satisfied with the car. After going through the measured mile at 120 mph and then at 170 mph, his only serious criticism was that the steering felt too direct and he asked for the ratio to be changed from 25:1 to 100:1, the lowest ratio available. He also wanted some of the cockpit switches repositioned so as to make them more accessible to him. All in all, everyone felt happy with the initial sorties.

Moreover, the American challenge did not seem to hold a serious threat unless it was from Mickey Thompson, who was still to be breaking records a decade later. Thompson, with a car powered by four supercharged Pontiac engines, did in fact record 406 mph on one run but had trouble on the return trip and retired from the flats to lick his wounds and return to fight another day.

Modifications complete, *Bluebird* was ready for further trials on September 15th. This time Donald did runs at 170 mph and 250 mph and laconically reported that the course was rough but the car handled extremely well. The plan was to step up runs by around 50 mph a time until car and driver were ready for the 'big one', and at this stage all was going according to plan.

Next morning at 4 a.m., the team rubbed the sleep from their eyes and went to the hangar where *Bluebird* was housed. The car was loaded on to its trailer and by 5 a.m. a ghostly convoy—trailer, refuelling vehicles, Landrovers and private Rovers, fire truck and so on—was winding through Wendover headed for the desert.

The first run would be towards the mountains and it was essential that it took place before the sun came up over those mountains, a happening scheduled for 6.15 a.m. You may be wondering why such an early start was necessary at all. The principal reason for it was that at that time of the day there was no wind. Donald arrived, raring to go, about 5.45 a.m. and soon after 6 made his first run, clocking 300 mph.

Delighted with the way things were going, he decided to make the next run an acceleration test. The car was turned round, refuelled and at 7.12 moved off, accelerating rapidly. Such quick acceleration would be essential if *Bluebird* were to take the record, since the course was about 11 miles along and it was estimated that the car must reach at least 300 mph in the first mile and a half of this stretch if the attempt was to be successful and the car brought safely to rest at the end of the course.

So off on his acceleration test went Donald. Travelling behind at a more circumspect 90 mph were two Rovers, amongst their occupants Tonia, Leo Villa, Ken Norris, Peter Carr and Tommy Wisdom. Suddenly they saw ahead a cloud of salt and a flashing blue object in the sky. In the sky? Yes, it was *Bluebird* which had quite literally taken off and was flying through the air.

(above) Donald Campbell and wife Tonia with the Segrave Trophy which he was awarded for his outstanding performance in raising his own water speed record in 1958. (*An RAC photo*)

(below) Three great Segrave Trophy winners: world champion motor-cyclist Geoff Duke, record-breaker Donald Campbell and ace Grand Prix driver Stirling Moss. (*Photo by Sport & General*)

The sad end of Donald's 1960 land record attempt at Bonneville: *Bluebird* immediately after the accident in which Donald was lucky to escape alive. (*Photo by Dunlop Rubber Co.*)

Bryan Cooper, who was Public Relations Officer for the project, described what happened: 'Within 1.6 miles of the start, the telemetry dials at the north pit showed that *Bluebird* had incredibly accelerated to a speed of 365 mph. At this point the car began to slide towards the left of the track. The cause of this was a combination of factors—the effect of a gushing crosswind, the bad condition of the salt on that part of the track [remember Leo Villa's comment?] and higher torque values than were anticipated, making it more difficult to prevent the wheels slipping. A difference in adhesion between the left and right wheels gave a rotational effect to the car and caused it to spin to the left side of the course. At a point 1.9 miles from the start, the right-hand wheels went into rough salt beyond the course and the car crashed over on its right side, almost at right angles to the course.

'With its length facing the wind like a huge aeroplane wing, *Bluebird* took off from the ground and twisted crazily into the air. That first, vicious twisting motion caused Campbell to lose consciousness. [Tommy Wisdom says that it was thought that something was wrong with the oxygen mixture being fed to Campbell. Pure oxygen has the effect of making you drunk.] He next remembers banging his head very hard and was then semi-conscious as the car rumbled to a halt and he was being pulled from the cockpit.

'After leaving the ground, *Bluebird* hurtled through the air for about 200 yards—four tons of metal travelling at over 350 mph. It touched down again on its tail, then on to its right wheels five yards further on. Three more times the car bounced to the ground within a distance of 70 yards, then went into a 200-yard S slide and came to a halt facing the direction it had come. Strewn over a wide area were pieces of twisted metalwork and also two of the huge tyres and wheels. Despite the tremendous impact when the car bounced, not one of the tyres burst.'

Cooper commented that no one who saw the accident believed that Campbell could possibly have survived it. Yet when Leo Villa reached the wreckage he was amazed to find that the cockpit canopy slid back easily and Donald was still

F

conscious although bleeding from an ear. It subsequently transpired that the design of the seating and cockpit structure combined with the safety harness the driver was wearing had protected him from injury until the moment when the car began to crab sideways. Then Donald's head had been rattled to and fro inside the canopy and a skull fracture, fortunately of not too serious a nature, resulted.

It was then that the critics who compared Donald unfavourably with his father received a short, sharp answer. From his hospital bed came the announcement that as soon as he was fit and the car was ready again, another attempt on the world record would be made. There was only one appropriate comment to make to that and it came in the form of a terse communique from Sir Alfred Owen, the millionaire industrialist whose firm had built the car. It was more eloquent than any long-winded eulogy and it said, in effect, that if the driver had the guts to try again, Owen would rebuild the car.

Thus the disappointment was eased and in the months of convalescence which followed Donald was able to plan ahead. As with his father before him, the question of a suitable course loomed large and Donald was having second thoughts about the salt flats of Utah. Besides, Australia tempted with a beckoning finger.

The car, on the other hand, presented few problems. The latest edition of *Bluebird*, crash or no crash, was a unique vehicle, the first car designed for a world land speed record attempt to use a gas turbine engine. This engine, the Bristol Siddeley Proteus 755, would be described by engineers as a free turbine but more popularly as a turbo-prop. It drove all four wheels of *Bluebird* and although no one realized it this too made it unique, for only one other car was to take the world land speed record and have direct drive from engine to wheels. *Bluebird* and her like were to be superseded by true jets, relying entirely on their tremendous power for propulsion and having no direct drive. There was to be a tremendous fluttering in the official dovecots before such records would be recognized.

But all of this was several years in the future as Donald Campbell lay in his hospital bed and surveyed the situation.

The rebuilt *Bluebird* would without doubt have potential enough to break John Cobb's long-standing record. At full throttle, the engine would deliver 4,250 horse-power and, always assuming full throttle could be used, this meant a top speed of around 500 mph. Moreover, on the ill-fated Bonneville expedition *Bluebird* had accelerated from a standstill to nearly 400 mph in 24 seconds over a distance of one and a half miles, with less than 80 per cent of full power being used.

The engine was, in fact, of the same type used to propel the fastest warships in the world at that time, the Royal Navy's Brave class patrol boats. Like all gas turbines of the type, it delivered high power for its bulk and weight, being just over eight feet long, 40 inches in diameter and weighing about 3,000 lb. It required no cooling system and no clutch because it used the equivalent of a fluid torque converter, the output shaft being coupled directly and permanently to bevel gears in the front and rear axles. The turbine provided no engine braking on the overrun at low speeds but at 400 mph about 500 h.p. would be available for braking if the throttle were closed.

In fact two braking systems provided the stopping power— air flaps opening out from the rear of the car and power-operated Girling disc brakes on all four wheels. The discs ran at a maximum temperature of 2,200°F—almost white hot.

The overall weight of the car was four tons. It measured 30 feet long, eight feet wide and four feet nine inches high without its removable tail fin. It ran on aviation turbine kerosene—and family motorists who complain about fuel consumption might like to know that at full speed *Bluebird* did one and a half miles to the gallon. All in all, quite a car, and as soon as Donald was out of hospital he began to supervise work on the rebuilding. With refinements and improvements it would be the most expensive and advanced car ever built and this time no fewer than 80 British firms had joined in a co-operative venture to bring back the record.

For Donald remained the question: the Bonneville Salt Flats again? or virgin territory in Australia?

Chapter Ten

Down Under—and Almost Out

AUSTRALIA IT WAS. The dry bed of Lake Eyre in South Australia offered 3,700 square miles of salt flats and on them a course of 16 miles was marked out, plenty of distance in which to accelerate, reach top speed and slow down again to a safe halt. But marking out the course was not a simple matter. Roads had to be constructed so that all the equipment and personnel could be brought up. The course itself had to be smoothed and the many little islands of salt removed. It all took time and although Campbell landed in Australia in March 1963, the course was not ready for trials until May. Meanwhile he occupied himself by exhibiting the car at the Melbourne Trade Fair and later at a multiple store in Adelaide.

It had not rained at Lake Eyre for seven years yet hardly had the course been cleared then down it came in torrents and in no time at all the stretch which had taken so much sweat and toil to produce was deep under flood water. Work started again. Again a course was ready. Then again—for the second time in seven years—it rained at Lake Eyre. The detractors were in full cry now, although how any man could be expected to combat the cruel luck of heavy rain in a spot which had been dry for seven years it is hard to imagine. Nor were the critics appeased by the fact that in between the showers Donald had eased *Bluebird* up to 250 mph in trials.

It was now July and the calm cooler weather of the Australian winter was fast running out. Campbell was not idle but flew to Western Australia. Desperate situations need desperate remedies and even at this late stage he seized on the remote chance that an alternative course might be found in the west. Meanwhile criticism in the press and elsewhere mounted, not the least kindly suggestion being that he had lost his nerve after the crash in Utah.

Perhaps the best face which can be put on it is that few people have first-hand knowledge and experience of the tremendous difficulties that confront the would-be record-breaker and from thousands of miles away (which is where the majority of Campbell's critics were) those difficulties, far from being magnified, tend to diminish. Newspapers following up the 'he's lost his nerve' theme developed the idea that perhaps another driver should supersede Campbell in what had now become apparently a 'nationalized' undertaking as far as Fleet Street was concerned. Racing drivers were interviewed and asked (by people who had no say in the matter) if they would be prepared to step into *Bluebird*'s cockpit when Campbell, either voluntarily or otherwise, vacated it. One top driver, Stirling Moss, was quoted as saying that Campbell lacked the split-second reactions of a Grand Prix driver. It was hardly an atmosphere calculated to cheer up the Campbell outfit as they watched months of work washed away by the pitiless rain.

Donald was probably less worried about the general run of press criticism than about the fact that there now appeared in the ranks of the opposition some of the people who were backing the venture. Chief amongst these was one of his principal sponsors, Sir Alfred Owen, who said that the *Bluebird* project had cost him nearly half a million pounds so far, that he had nothing to show for it and was bitterly disappointed.

It was the final straw for a tense and frustrated Campbell. All further efforts were abandoned and as the team made preparations for the return home, Donald issued writs for slander against Sir Alfred and claimed heavy damages. In all the long association of Malcolm and Donald Campbell with record-breaking on land and water there had rarely, if ever, been a moment as wounding and heart-breaking as this. A venture in which all had embarked with high hopes, high ideals, with brains, energy and money, and with pride, had foundered on acres of desert which even the aborigines did not want and now looked like being extinguished entirely in the squalid wranglings of the court-room.

In the sequel, both Sir Alfred and Donald proved themselves bigger men than that. Not much was ever printed about what happened when the two came face to face upon Donald's return to England, but most people must have been relieved when Sir Alfred terminated speculation with the comment, 'We are going to work together again'.

Nevertheless, Sir Alfred had not been the only one of Donald's backers to become disillusioned with the lack of progress of the project. He had attracted the headlines as the most powerful man behind the scenes but there were other sponsors on a smaller scale who expressed their disapproval in a positive fashion by withdrawing their support from any future attempts which might be made.

So it was that in February 1964 Donald Campbell and *Bluebird* and, not least, Tonia returned to Australia, minus a great many supporters and with some heavy holes in Donald's own personal bank account where he had had to bear a great deal of the expenses himself. If ever there was a time in Donald Campbell's career when he proved himself a man to rank with his father this was it: not because of what he achieved but because of what he endured. Where people met and talked about such things his name was almost a joke. An atmosphere had been created in which many people dismissed his efforts as futile, a quick method of throwing money and effort away.

The *Bluebird* team thought otherwise. Although there must have been many days when everyone from Donald downwards must, at least inwardly, have thought that the critics were right, they kept slogging away. There were nights when, after the evening meal, they sat around in the open under the vast expanse of Australian sky just like pioneers of the West on a wagon train moving towards the promised land. But in their case it rather looked as if the promised land might be unattainable. Throughout all these trying and anxious times, Tonia was by Donald's side, working with a will, helping with the cooking and laundering under the strangest circumstances any housewife could imagine.

The weeks slipped by. Oceans and continents away in Britain, the name of Donald Campbell was almost forgotten. Then, suddenly, came the news that conditions seemed right and he was at last ready to make an all-out bid to smash

John Cobb's record and become the first man to push the figures beyond the 400 mph mark.

Shortly after sunrise on July 17th, 1964, *Bluebird* was wheeled out on to the lake-bed. A noticeable cross-wind was blowing across the track and the gauge indicated a strength of about 2 mph, sufficient to be a hazard to a projectile travelling at the speed of *Bluebird* and just about the maximum windspeed permissible with safety. To Donald it was just another minor irritant and one which would certainly not prevent him having a long-delayed stab at the record.

With everything ready, the big moment arrived. Donald snugged down into the cockpit and away went the giant car. Quickly it built up speed and then, as it grew smaller in the distance, there came a heart-stopping moment. *Bluebird* veered towards the right hand side of the track, obviously caught in a gust from the cross-wind. But it was only a momentary alarm, as Campbell straightened the car out and went smoothly on his way. Then came the wait for news from the timekeepers. When it came it was good. The speed through the measured mile was 403.1 mph and through the kilometre 388.7. Although not so good as hoped for it meant that Campbell had only to make the return journey at a similar speed in order to have broken Cobb's mark of 394.196 mph.

Break it he did. As the huge car rolled to a stop at the end of the return run, Campbell stepped out, hugged Tonia and said, 'Darling, we've made it'. Then came the official timings. The speed over the mile was absolutely identical with that on the first run—403.1, whilst over the kilometre Campbell had been a little faster on the return trip at 400.5. As the news was announced, spectators cheered and members of his team, not to mention the Australian Army, rushed forward to chair Campbell in triumph.

It was a happy ending but it might have been a grim one. The sharp salt crystals were hard on tyres and when *Bluebird* was inspected the tread on one tyre had been torn right down to the fabric. Officials going over the course found lumps of rubber from the tyres 'the size of matchboxes'.

When the cheering and the excitement died down there came a time for cool, clinical appraisal of the situation, a time to say 'Where do we go from here?' Back in Britain, Sir Alfred Owen was quoted as saying: 'I am thrilled that at last it has been achieved. I send my heartiest congratulations. I expect that I shall be telephoning him in the morning.'

The praise from many quarters was muted. Truly it was a remarkable thing to have done but Cobb's record had stood for 17 years and now, despite all the money and effort which had been lavished on Donald's attempts, he had succeeded in bettering Cobb's figures by only nine miles an hour. In the blasé world of the sixties, the cynics remained remarkably unimpressed. One newspaper saw fit to put a footnote on its report of the attempt to the effect that at the end of the war the latest German fighter had a speed of 428 mph and the latest Spitfire at that time could do 450 mph. What precisely that had to do with the world land speed record presumably only the ingenious sub-editor knew.

Campbell himself confessed to being heartbroken that he did not beat the 407.45 mph which American Craig Breedlove's three-wheeled jet car *Spirit of the Age* had reached on the Bonneville Salt Flats the previous August. Breedlove's speed had not been officially recognized—apart from anything else, the 'car', having only three wheels, was technically a 'motorcycle'—but Campbell felt that his new record would have achieved more recognition if it had effectively disposed of the Breedlove figures as well as Cobb's undisputed mark. Moreover, the odds were that Breedlove would still further improve his figures during attempts planned for the next few weeks.

But the Campbell team had another card to play. In London, David Wynne-Morgan, the project controller, announced that Campbell would follow up his land speed record with another attempt to break the world water speed record. Mr. Wynne-Morgan said, moreover, that the attempt would be made that year. No one had ever set a world land speed record and a world water speed record in the same year, 'not even Donald's father'. He added that the land record had cost £1 million (not £2 million as reported in some quarters).

The record run had been made in appalling conditions and 'if it wasn't for the fact that all these delays made some people think his nerve had gone I don't think Donald would have made that attempt on that track in that condition'. He added that the water speed attack might be made at Lake Hindmarsh, in Victoria, Australia, in September. The hydroplane was already in Australia.

After the water speed record, Campbell planned to build a jet-propelled car to go faster than *Bluebird* and believed that speeds up to 700 mph were possible. At Lake Eyre, Ken Norris, designer of *Bluebird*, commented: 'It will not just be a jet engine on wheels. We have a surprise for the Americans and everyone else.' The new design was already on the drawing-boards and Donald said the idea was an exciting one. To some it all sounded like whistling in the dark. There was a tremendous gap between 403 mph and 700 mph and whilst the new *Bluebird* project was taking shape, the Americans, officially recognized or not, were doing their best to plug that gap. Tom Green, driving the pure jet, four-wheeled *Wingfoot Express*, clocked 413.2 mph in October and Art Arfons followed up with 434.2 mph. It began to look as if Donald would need 700 mph by the time his new car was ready.

Meanwhile the water speed record monopolized his attention. Lake Dumbleyung in Western Australia was finally settled upon as the scene of the attempt but for a time it seemed that the misfortunes which had followed Donald's land attempts would still haunt him on water. The weeks slipped away and 1964 drew to a close. Since a major aspect of the attempt was to achieve what had never been done before—the land and water records in one year—Donald and his helpers began to feel desperate.

December did, however, bring one piece of encouraging news when the FIA, controlling body of automobilism, and the FIM, which performed a similar function for the world of motorcycling, finally cleared up the confusions and ambiguities created by pure jets and three-wheelers and jointly laid down new definitions for the world land speed record. For the first time, an official land speed record was recognized by both FIA and FIM. It was open to any vehicle which depended on the ground for its support during its record run and which was steered by a driver in the vehicle who could also control acceleration and deceleration. Four-wheel attempts would be controlled by the FIA and three-or two-wheel attempts by the FIM. The best performance by a *normal* automobile or motor-cycle, irrespective of class, would be known as world records.

These rulings meant that Campbell's *Bluebird* was still an official world record holder. But it was hardly very helpful to him as he and Tonia and Leo Villa sat and watched the winds sweep across the surface of Lake Dumbleyung and the leaves of December fell from the calendar in swift succession. The last day of the month dawned and with it the final hope of setting both records in one year. All the odds seemed against it and so desperate was Donald that he even contemplated at this late hour finding another lake where the water might be smoother. Then suddenly, in early afternoon, Dumbleyung calmed. It seemed like a miracle and to Campbell it was the half-chance he needed. He raced for *Bluebird*, shouting at Leo Villa, 'Let's go, let's go'.

It was a gamble and one which nearly ended in disaster. Donald thought his last moments had come as he roared over the lake at more than 280 mph. Crackling over the two-way radio, his voice screamed, 'I've bought it, I've bought it, I'm going in'. A patch of rough water had buffeted *Bluebird* off course and he had to struggle frantically to bring the boat under control. But he managed to do so and streaked across the rippling surface to register 283.6 mph over the measured kilometre.

Less than two minutes later he was on the way back for the second run and this time the water was even rougher. With victory almost within his grasp, the cruel fates which seemed to pursue him chose to strike again.

Halfway through the approach for the second run, the engines cut out. He was faced with the choice of going back to the start again, which would have meant refuelling, or restarting and attempting the second run with a much shorter approach in which to work up speed. He chose the latter course and the gamble was justified. As he shot across the measured kilometre he yelled into the microphone 'What's my speed?' and the answer came back '269 mph'. The combined speeds gave an average of 276.33 mph, breaking Donald's own record set some five years before on Lake Coniston by 16 miles an hour. He had become the first man in history to capture both land and water records in one year.

Tonia was so excited that as the boat neared the landing-stage pontoon she leaped into the water and swam out to her husband. As she embraced him, Donald gave her the St. Christopher medal, originally given to him by his father, which he had been wearing.

By the time *Bluebird* was moored alongside the pontoon, Donald's excitement and elation had given way to emotion. He said, 'Boys, this is the eve of the old skipper's death sixteen years ago'. The entire crew and the watching spectators stood for a minute in silent salute to the memory of Sir Malcolm Campbell.

Afterwards Donald told reporters: 'We were very lucky. A quarter of an hour after the last run there was a 25-knot wind blowing. It started about the time I made the second run but I was able to squeeze the return run in before it bothered me too much.' He added that he was now going to relax and spend a lengthy holiday with his wife, Tonia, who, despite losing their expected child earlier in the year, had scarcely left her husband's side during all his trials and tribulations. 'She has been a tower of strength and support for all this,' said Donald. 'People ask how she feels. I'm reminded often of what President Eisenhower said after I crashed at Bonneville Salt Flats. He looked at the scene and said: "If I had to get involved with all this, I'd rather be in the driver's seat than watching from the lakeside." '

Tonia said that she didn't know if she could go through it all again. But she did, of course. In Sydney, on the way home, the lovely cabaret star said her husband would make no more record attempts for at least a year. People had been sneering at him and claiming he was 'chicken', she said. On the waters of Lake Dumbleyung, he had given them their answer.

The Segrave Awarding Committee in London expressed their opinion of Campbell's unique achievement by once again awarding him their trophy. The nation was more grudging in its praise, his only official honour the CBE. But for Donald the reward had been in silencing the knockers and not letting 'the old skipper' down.

Chapter Eleven

The Americans

THERE WERE TIMES in the whirling twenties when record-breakers like Segrave and Malcolm Campbell had the field virtually to themselves. Those days were long gone. Whilst Donald Campbell fought to achieve the double in Australia, challengers for the land speed record proliferated. All the world (or at least that part of it which spoke with an American accent) and his wife (in one case, quite literally) had designs on the title of 'Fastest man on earth'. Mickey Thompson and the ill-fated Athol Graham were fleetingly on our scene earlier. Now came a couple of feuding brothers, Walter and Art Arfons, the swift Craig Breedlove and, not least, a gentleman named Bob Summers. Breedlove, Walter Arfons (with his drivers Tom Green and Bob Patroe) and Art Arfons had all achieved much whilst Campbell was busy elsewhere and now 1965 looked like being the big year. The December decision of the FIA and the FIM meant that there were two records to be broken: Campbell's 403 in a normal automobile and Art Arfons' 434 in a jet with power not transmitted directly to the wheels.

The assortment of cars out to break these records was quite the most fantastic ever assembled. Only one, however, was a conventional car, if conventional is ever a word which can be applied to a land speed record-breaker, and this was *Goldenrod*, pride and joy of the Summers brothers and driven by Bob Summers. *Goldenrod* had direct drive to the wheels whereas all the other potential speed merchants were pure jets with no direct link between power and wheels.

Trail-blazer of the new jet age had been Walter Arfons, who was nearing fifty and subject to heart attacks. Forced to relinquish the wheel by ill-health he had concentrated on building drag-racers and developing young drivers to handle them. The previous year his *Wingfoot Express* had clocked over 413 mph at Bonneville, a glory which was short-lived because brother Arthur in his aptly named *Green Monster*, one of the ugliest cars ever built for the record, beat this figure comfortably only three days later, both efforts causing heartburn to Donald Campbell in far-off Australia. Piquancy was added to the situation because the Arfons, who were actually half-brothers, did not get along too well together. The disagreement was further exacerbated by the fact that they used different makes of tyre, Walter being sponsored by Goodyear and Arthur by Firestone.

The brothers had more to worry about than family rivalry, however. Craig Breedlove, a 27-year-old Californian, returned from the West in his three-wheeled *Spirit of America* to register first 468.72 mph and then the fantastic figure of 526.28 mph in the course of which he wrecked his vehicle. Back to the salt flats came Art Arfons and the *Green Monster* to return 536.71— and that car too was somewhat the worse for wear at the end of the attempt. Now it was big brother Walter's turn to have another crack, this time with the aid of three jet-assist take-off rockets. But the rains came down and it was back to the garages for the winter for all the record men.

That was in 1964. Now it was another year and the competition looked like being hotter than ever.

Breedlove set the ball rolling. On November 2nd in his new *Spirit of America* he beat Art Arfons' time by almost 19 mph. The *Spirit* was a beautifully streamlined machine looking very much like the fuselage of an aircraft, complete to pointed nose and tailplane. Depending upon one's point of view, it was also described as 'a needle-nosed Coca-cola bottle with a tail fin'. Either way it was designed with lurking thoughts about the sound barrier. It was now an automobile instead of a motor-cycle, the three-wheel lay-out of the original having been replaced by the more conventional four wheels. The J79 engine exerted a thrust of 15,000 pounds and so, as with most of the would-be record-breakers, a parachute was needed to assist the normal braking system in slowing the car down safely. *Spirit of America* was sponsored by Goodyear.

The record did not come easily to Breedlove. His early trial runs showed that the vehicle frame needed strengthening. That was done and on the next trial air pressure caved in the nose. That fault was fixed—and the next time the car went out of control at 600 mph, eventually coming safely to rest ominously near the spot where Breedlove had crashed the year before. But after a month of such trials and tribulations, the man from Los Angeles tooled over the salt flats at an average speed of 555.483 mph.

He held the record for exactly five days.

Art Arfons, the former star of the hot-rod circuits, with a vehicle that was described variously as 'the ugliest and cheapest ever built', 'as ungainly as a garbage truck', and by many other choice tags, showed that his salt flats performances of the previous year were no fluke and that it would take something extra-special to rob him permanently of his crown. As for the criticisms of the *Green Monster* and its appearance, Art loved the car like a mother loves her child. It was even suggested that he insisted on his crew giving it an affectionate kiss each day. If so the car, powered with a jet engine from an aircraft, certainly responded to affection. Breedlove's figures were obliterated as Arfons clocked an average of 576.55 mph, making the *Green Monster* the fastest garbage-truck in the world. American journalists reported at the time that Arfons was in a hurry because his wife was expecting their third child and he did not want to waste time lingering on the salt flats.

In fact, he could not have stayed on the salt flats even if he had wanted to since once again the car suffered damage on its record-breaking run. The new machines were bringing with them new hazards. On this occasion, with the car travelling at nearly 600 mph, the right rear tyre blew out (the condition of the salt was said to be very rough) and the cockpit, located to one side of the car, filled with smoke. Arfons slowed to about 250 mph, at which speed he was able to rip the cockpit canopy open, but the car suffered damage which necessitated transporting it back to the garage.

Arfons, incidentally, blamed the engine and not the tyre for the blow-out, saying that failure of the afterburner put an extra

load on the tyre concerned. Technical experts have confessed
themselves puzzled by this since there is no direct connection
between engine and wheels, but, as one of them was quoted,
'Since no one else has driven a car at such a speed, it is difficult
to dispute him'.

Someone else, however, was about to drive a car at such a
speed. Breedlove was determined not to let the record go
without a struggle. Pessimists looked at the gathering rain-
clouds and recalled that the last time a record-breaker had
made a successful run on the salt flats as late in the year as this
was in 1937, the man concerned being Captain George Eyston.
It rained on Sunday, November 14th, 1965, and left puddles of
water at one end of the course. The pessimists shook their heads
and said 'I told you so'. Breedlove remained apparently
unconvinced of the hopelessness of his cause, so much so that he
brought his car out for a run later in the day but was turned
down by United States Auto Club officials who declared that
the winds were too high for an attempt to be made with com-
parative safety. Still not deterred, Breedlove and his crew were
on the flats next morning at seven. The wind, although still
frisky, had dropped considerably and the sky was clearing.

Soon after 8 a.m., *Spirit of America* streaked northwards over
the 11-mile course and registered 593.18 mph. Three-quarters
of an hour later, Breedlove made the return journey and this
time really whooped it up with a speed of 608.20 mph, giving
him an average for the two runs of 600.69 mph. It was no mean
feat, especially when one realizes that the first part of the return
run was made over that section of the course which was under
water.

Breedlove joked about it afterwards: 'We were going real
slow at that point.' 'How slow?' asked a reporter. 'About
300 mph,' said the straight-faced Breedlove.

That was it for the year in terms of ultimate speed. Arfons
and his *Green Monster* were back East and Breedlove and his
Spirit of America had perforce to rest on their laurels.

Overshadowed by the Arfons versus Breedlove duel had
been a striking effort from the Summers brothers, an effort
which broke Donald Campbell's official world record for

(above) So salt lakes are flat! Close-up of a salt 'island' on Lake Eyre with a 12-inch ruler to show the scale. These islands must be levelled before a fast run is possible. (*Photo by Dunlop Rubber Co.*)

(below) One of *Bluebird's* wheels immediately after Donald's 1960 accident. In spite of severe punishment, only one tyre was found to have lost any air, and that was because the wheel had been damaged by taking the full weight of the four-ton car. (*Photo by Dunlop Rubber Co.*)

(above) Close-up action of Donald Campbell in one of his earlier—and unsuccessful—world water speed record attempts. (*Photo by Kemsley Newspapers*)

(below) Wake of the *Bluebird*. Donald's 1950 attempt at Coniston which ended with the engine 'blowing up' and the shattering news that America's Stanley Sayers had captured the record. (*Photo by 'Daily Express'*)

'normal' automobiles. Like Arfons, Bob and Bill Summers were hot-rodders with a lot of experience on the salt flats. Like Breedlove, they came from the Los Angeles area. Like Donald Campbell, they were imbued with the idea of holding the world land speed record. They had given a glimpse of what they might accomplish as far back as 1962 when they built a Chrysler-engined streamlined projectile which clocked 323 mph on the flats. It gave them a sense of direction. Bill worked as a truck-driver to finance them both while Bob devoted his time to turning out the record-breaker of their dreams.

Their efforts were impressive enough to encourage a modicum of support from Chrysler, Mobil, Firestone and a speed equipment manufacturer named Hurst. It wasn't very much in relation to world speed attempts but it helped. On November 11th, *Goldenrod*, a low-slung beauty which for looks and line challenged Segrave's *Golden Arrow* as the most eye-pleasing record contender of all time, was ready to roll. Bob Summers took it through the measured strip and notched up more than 400 mph. It was encouraging but Campbell's record was due for a reprieve. *Goldenrod* had wheel-bearing trouble and couldn't make the return journey necessary for the record.

Next morning the car was ready for another try. What happened was described laconically by the news agencies: 'American driver Bob Summers today broke Donald Campbell's world record for wheel-drive cars. He drove his 32-feet needle-shaped car, *Goldenrod*, to set a new mark of 409 mph at Bonneville Salt Flats, Utah. Campbell's record of 403 mph was set up last year at Lake Eyre, South Australia. In London, Donald Campbell revealed that he had received an American offer to build his projected faster-than-sound rocket car. He said: "A New York syndicate has made the offer. If we go ahead the car will be British-engined, British-designed, British-driven, but it would be American-made." '

Dreams maybe. But an American truck-driver and his brother, nursing such a dream, had just taken the world record with a speed of 412.70 mph in one direction and 405.91 in the other. As Leo Levine wrote in *Autocar*, 'Not bad for a truck-

G

driver, a machinist and an idea'. Perhaps too there was an indication that money alone was not enough. The Summers project, it was said, cost a quarter of a million dollars, the estimates on Campbell's *Bluebird* project varied between three and ten million dollars. Sponsors were said to have invested half a million dollars in Breedlove, only fifty thousand in Arfons. Whatever the financial rights and wrongs of the situation, 1965 ended with Breedlove undisputed 'king' and Bob Summers undoubted holder of what had always previously been known as the world land speed record.

Arfons said he would be back next year—and he was. Campbell said that he was still undecided about his project to take to jets himself and attempt to beat the speed of sound at more than 840 mph. 'The American achievements are a tremendous challenge to Britain,' he was reported as saying, 'but whether or not I will proceed with my own plans I have not yet decided. We have already been working for about a year on the project but there are many factors involved such as the considerable number of business affairs in which I am now engaged.'

A sideshow during the struggle on the salt flats in 1965 had been the 'women's world speed record'. It may not be officially recognized but before any male drivers scoff just take a look at the facts. On September 27th, Betty Skelton, driving an Arfons-designed car *Cyclops*, turned in 277.62 mph. On November 4th, Mrs. Breedlove tooled *Spirit of America* along at 308.56 mph. Beat that if you can, you daredevil 40-mile-an-hour commuter!

For Donald Campbell it must have been a bitterly disappointing year. When record-breaking at Bonneville had been confined to the non-wheel-driven efforts of Walter and Arthur Arfons and Craig Breedlove, there had always been the consolation that these were not conventional cars and indeed, as someone suggested, one might just as well say that the world land speed record was held by the American Air Force jet sled which ran on rails. Now the Summers brothers and *Goldenrod* had put the issue beyond argument by breaking Campbell's mark in a 'normal' car. However bold a face Donald might put on matters, it seemed likely that Bob Summers would go down in the record books as the last holder of the world record for wheel-driven cars. It did not seem probable that anyone would devote the money and time to building another contender when inevitably the headlines would be stolen by the much faster pure jets of Breedlove, Arfons & Co. Sponsors are not, after all, in the record-breaking business for their health.

Winter laid its icy grip on the Western world and, as the year drew to its final curtain, no further word came of Campbell and his project. In the relentless pace of the modern world, it could hardly be said that news was awaited with bated breath.

Epilogue

The Deeds Remain

THE MONTHS WHICH FOLLOWED Donald's 'two-in-one' achievement brought mixed rewards. One of his sponsors produced a film in colour of the 1964 land and water records which graphically illustrated the measure of Campbell's effort. One had the feeling that if it had been possible for the film to have a wider audience there might have been a readier appreciation of the worth of those efforts. Meanwhile Donald and Tonia led a life much like most other couples with Donald popping off to the office instead of soaring over the salt flats. In spite of the critics, he was in demand as an after-dinner speaker and as a 'fund raiser' at charity functions.

He widened the scope of his business ventures—not always, it must be admitted, with conspicuous success. But there were moments, as when he received the Segrave Trophy for a history-making third time, when the magic world of record-breaking came near again and the adrenalin started working in the Campbell glands. It was not to be expected that Donald could ever tear himself completely away from fast cars and fast boats. The dark suit and umbrella with which he was from time to time to be seen in Pall Mall might indicate 'businessman' to the stranger, but to those who knew him it seemed a thin disguise for a man of action.

The prospects of another attempt at the land record seemed fairly remote, however. *Bluebird* was still in running order but it was highly unlikely that her performance could be improved upon to an extent sufficient to make another bid feasible. At the same time, there was a noticeable lack of wealthy sponsors prepared to dig deep into their vaults to build the new project which Donald and his helpers had in mind.

The doubts and uncertainties about a land record bid were

soon to be resolved in highly dramatic fashion. Donald had
agreed to give a demonstration run in *Bluebird* for charity, the
venue being the RAF station at Debden, Essex. When the day
came he was not too well, but rather than let the organizers
down he agreed that someone else might drive the car. The
'someone' was a very experienced competition driver but, alas,
was not familiar with that special breed of automobile used in
record-breaking. The short painful end to the demonstration
run came with a pile-up which resulted in damage to the tune
of £50,000—and the car was not insured. It was the end of
Bluebird and, as events were to transpire, the end of Donald's
quest for land speed honours.

There remained 'sister' *Bluebird*, the boat which had been
in store at Hounslow since breaking the water record 20 months
previously. The hull was 10 years old, the engine 15—a slender
and ageing foundation on which to build another attempt. But
if Donald Campbell's career had shown just one thing it was
surely a determination not to be put off by difficulties. Another
magic milestone loomed in his mind—to be the first man to
beat 300 mph on water—and without more ado the team set to
work again. Bristol-Siddeley agreed to loan an Orpheus jet
engine and that was the main headache solved. By November
8th, 1966, the boat was ready. The rest of the story was
written in the newspaper headlines of five continents.

On July 19th, 1967, Mrs. Donald Campbell was presented
with the Segrave Trophy posthumously awarded to her
husband 'for the inspiring example of courage, initiative and
skill which he gave to his fellow countrymen, and on their behalf
to the world, during his life and in the record attempt in which
he met his death in January 1967, and in recognition of his
outstanding contribution in the fields of mechanical develop-
ment and aerodynamics'.

The presentation was made at a ceremony in the Great
Gallery of the Royal Automobile Club during which members
of Donald Campbell's team were also honoured. Gold medals
were presented to K. W. and L. H. Norris, the *Bluebird* designers;
Leo Villa, chief operational engineer; Maurice W. Parfitt and
Anthony E. James, engineering and technical; and J. L.

Stollery, hydrodynamics and aerodynamics. Framed copies of the citation went to Louis Goossens, in charge of radio communications and refuelling facilities; Kenneth Reaks, instruments; and Kenneth A. Pearson and Jack Lavis, engine specialists.

In October of the same year, there was almost a full turnout of members of the K7 Club, the 80 people who had been most closely associated with Donald in his record-breaking adventures, at their first meeting since his tragic accident. The following month, Leo Villa was invested with the OBE for services to land and water speed records. 'You have been with the Campbell family for a good many years I think?' said the Queen. 'Forty-five years, ma'am,' replied Villa.

The echoes of those 45 years were not yet stilled. In January 1968, Michael Brennan, of the *Sun* newspaper, was named News Photographer of the Year for his pictures of Donald's last fateful run. A few days later wreaths were placed on Lake Coniston opposite the spot where the accident had taken place. Donald's mother, Lady Campbell, laid a wreath of roses on the water and another of red carnations on behalf of his widow, Tonia, who was in America. There was a happier postscript in July when Donald's 22-year-old daughter, Georgina, married farmer Clifford Percy at Partridge Green in Sussex.

Craig Breedlove, holder of the world land speed record, was sued for divorce by the girl who had shared his triumphs on the salt flats. Despite his domestic troubles, however, he prepared for an attempt on Bob Summer's wheel-driven record with a new car, similar in layout to his three-wheeled jet but with four wheels to qualify as a car, not a motor-cycle combination. The front wheels in this case were placed very close together in the nose of the machine so that in external appearance it looked little different from the three-wheeler. It was powered with a supercharged, fuel-injected American Motors AMX unit developing 1,000 brake horse-power which Breedlove said was sufficient to break 425 mph.

Meanwhile, the veteran Mickey Thompson had returned to the salt flats with the same objective as Breedlove. His attempt nearly ended in disaster. At more than 350 mph a tyre burst and the 30-foot-long car started to spin off the course towards a control building. Thompson regained control by switching off the rear engine, which is supercharged and drives the rear wheels only, and accelerating the front engine. Afterwards he said, 'If I'd been watching, I'd have bet 1,000 dollars that the car would have flipped'. Wet weather put an end to further attempts.

Another message from the States reported that Donald's widow, Tonia, was to resume her singing career in New York and would tour America with the famous Guy Lombardo Orchestra. Lombardo's other claim to fame was—as a speedboat racer.

A gentleman called Lee Taylor came to London to attend a dinner in his honour given by the Royal Motor Yacht Club. Around the time Donald Campbell had been setting a new water record on Lake Dumbleyung, Taylor had been testing his speedboat, the *Hustler*, on a lake in Arizona. *Hustler* finished half way up a mountain and Taylor fractured his skull in three places, as well as sustaining an eye laceration. As if this were not enough, the helicopter which 'rescued' him dropped into the lake, crushing his left ankle. This might have been enough to deter any man, yet in June 1968 Lee Taylor clocked 285.213 mph on Guntersville Lake, Alabama, and took the record which had been so long in the Campbell family.

As he sat in his place of honour on the night of November 8th, 1968, Lady Campbell, Donald's mother, was preparing for a sentimental journey to Coniston, where wayside seats and newly planted trees mark Donald Campbell's last memorial. The plaque unveiled by his mother on November 10th reads, 'In memory of Donald Campbell, CBE, Queen's Commendation for Brave Conduct, who died on January 4th, 1967, while attempting to raise his own world water speed record on Coniston Water'.

Posterity will remember his achievements. No son ever strode harder to emulate a famous father, no son ever came nearer to achieving his desire. The speculation, the criticism, the carping, cannot take that away from Donald Campbell. Leo Villa, the man who knew him best, said in a memoir: 'I can absolutely refute the suggestion that Donald was a man with a death-wish. No one enjoyed life more. I do think that at the end of his life Donald was, to some extent, a disillusioned man. He expected more backing for his last attempt than he got, more keenness and enthusiasm from outside, and he was upset at not getting it.'

A profile in the *Daily Mail* said: 'Some people considered him an anachronism trying to break speed records on an English lake when spacemen were circling the Earth. But for Campbell this was his life. And his death.'

If Donald Campbell was an anachronism, then perhaps the world could do with more of them. Because without men like Malcolm Campbell and his son Donald, precious little would ever be achieved.

Father and son have gone; their deeds remain.

Appendix A: The Records

Malcolm Campbell

Land

September 25th, 1924: Pendine Sands, Wales: 146.16 mph
July 21st, 1925: Pendine Sands, Wales: 150.87 mph
February 4th, 1927: Pendine Sands, Wales: 174.88 mph
February 19th, 1928: Daytona Beach, USA: 206.96 mph
February 5th, 1931: Daytona Beach, USA: 246.09 mph
February 24th, 1932: Daytona Beach, USA: 253.97 mph
February 22nd, 1933: Daytona Beach, USA: 272.46 mph
March 7th, 1935: Daytona Beach, USA: 276.82 mph
September 3rd, 1935: Bonneville Salt Flats, USA: 301.13 mph

Water

September 1st, 1937: Lake Maggiore, Italy: 128.30 mph
September 2nd, 1937: Lake Maggiore, Italy: 129.50 mph
September 4th, 1938: Lake Hallwill, Switzerland: 130.94 mph
August 19th, 1939: Lake Coniston, England: 141.74 mph

Donald Campbell

Land

July 17th, 1964: Lake Eyre, Australia: 403.10 mph

Water

July 23rd, 1955: Lake Ullswater, England: 202.32 mph
November 16th, 1955: Lake Mead, Nevada, USA: 216.25 mph
September 19th, 1956: Lake Coniston, England: 225.63 mph
November 7th, 1957: Lake Coniston, England: 239.07 mph
November 10th, 1958: Lake Coniston, England: 248.62 mph
May 14th, 1959: Lake Coniston, England: 260.35 mph
December 31st, 1964: Lake Dumbleyung, Australia: 276.33 mph

H

Appendix B: The Segrave Trophy

In memory of the late Sir Henry Segrave. Awarded by a committee including representatives of the Royal Aero Club, the Newspaper Proprietors Association, the Royal Aeronautical Society, the Institution of Mechanical Engineers and the Royal Yachting Association, under the chairmanship of the Marquess Camden of the Royal Automobile Club. 'For the British subject who accomplishes the most outstanding demonstration of the possibilities of transport by land, air or water.'

1930: Air Commodore Sir Charles Kingsforth-Smith
1931: Squadron-Leader H. J. L. Hinkler, AFC, DSM
1932: Mrs. J. A. Mollison (Amy Johnson)
1933: Captain Sir Malcolm Campbell, MBE
1934: Mr. K. H. Waller
1935: Captain G. E. T. Eyston, OBE, MC
1936: Miss Jean Batten
1937: Flying-Officer A. E. Clouston
1938: Major A. T. Goldie Gardner
1939: Captain Sir Malcolm Campbell, MBE
1940 to 1945: Not awarded
1946: Mr. Geoffrey Raoul de Havilland, OBE
1947: Mr. John Rhodes Cobb
1948: Mr. John Douglas Derry, DFC
1949: Not awarded
1950: Not awarded
1951: Mr. Geoffrey Duke
1952: Not awarded
1953: Squadron-Leader Neville Duke, DSO, OBE, DFC, AFC
1954: Not awarded
1955: Mr. Donald Campbell
1956: Mr. Peter Twiss
1957: Mr. Stirling Moss
1958: Mr. Donald Campbell
1959: Not awarded
1960: Mr. Tom Brooke-Smith
1961: Not awarded

1962: Mr. W. Bedford, OBE, AFC
1963: Not awarded
1964: Mr. Donald Campbell
1965: Not awarded
1966: Mr. Donald Campbell (posthumous)
1967: Not awarded
1968: Wing Commander Kenneth Wallis

Bibliography

Malcolm Campbell, *Thunder Ahead*, Cassell, 1934
Henry Birkin, *Full Throttle*, Foulis, 1943
G. E. T. Eyston, *Fastest On Earth*, Floyd Clymer, 1946
W. Boddy, *Brooklands*, 1948
C. C. Wakefield & Co., *The Romance of Wakefields*, 1949
Malcolm Campbell, *Speed On Wheels*, Sampson Low, Marston, 1949
Laurence H. Cade, *The Modern World Book of Motors*, Sampson Low, Marston, 1950
Castrol Ltd., *Achievements*, 1951-67
W. Boddy, *The World's Land Speed Record*, Motor Racing Publications, 1951
Dorothy, Lady Campbell, *Malcolm Campbell, The Man As I Knew Him*, Hutchinson, 1951
Phil Drackett, *Motor Racing*, Foyles Handbooks, 1952
S. C. H. Davis, *The John Cobb Story*, Foulis, 1952
Richard Hough, *Tourist Trophy*, Hutchinson, 1957
Phil Drackett, *Great Moments In Motoring*, Phoenix House, 1958
Hugh Tours, *Parry Thomas, Designer-Driver*, Batsford, 1959
Cyril Posthumus, *Sir Henry Segrave*, Batsford, 1961
Lord Montagu of Beaulieu, *The Gordon Bennett Races*, Cassell, 1963
Herbert Jenkins, *BP Book of World Land Speed Records*, 1963
Phil Drackett, *Let's Look At Motor Cars*, Frederick Muller, 1966
Ross and Norris McWhirter (ed.), *Great Moments In Sport*, Vernons, 1967
Leo Villa, *The Donald Campbell Story*, Beaverbrook Newspapers, 1968
Also the files and records of the Royal Automobile Club, *Autocar, Motor, Sports Illustrated* and various national newspapers

Index

Iyŏ Island

IYŎ ISLAND

Chong Han-sook

translated by
Chun Kyung-ja

Si-sa-yong-o-sa, Inc., Korea
Pace International Research, Inc., U.S.A.

Published simultaneously in KOREA and the UNITED STATES

KOREA EDITION
First printing 1986
Si-sa-yong-o-sa, Inc.
55-1 Chongno 2-ga, Chongno-gu
Seoul 110, Korea

PL 992.2
H 3
I 913x

U.S. EDITION
First printing 1986
Pace International Research, Inc.
Tide Avenue, Falcon Cove
P.O. Box 51, Arch Cape
Oregon 97102, U.S.A.

ISBN: 0-87296-029-3

This book is a co-publication by Si-sa-yong-o-sa, Inc.
and The International Communication Foundation.

Preface

Our author, Professor Chung Han-sook, who has taught Korean literature at Korea University for over thirty years, was born in 1921 in North Pyongan Province and moved out of the Soviet Zone to the South soon after Liberation in 1945. By the time the present work appeared in 1960, he had already established a reputation as a writer through the publication of prose fiction and a play. The novella presented here in translation, *Iyŏ Island*, expresses a mature artistic sensibility which draws upon Professor Chung's sustained experimentation with prose techniques during the 1950s, a period in which modern Korean fiction began to grow increasingly self-conscious of the uniqueness and power of the vernacular tongue as an artistic instrument. In the intervening years, Professor Chung has been a prolific writer, producing scores of prose works, ranging from historical novels to short stories.

Iyŏ Island immediately struck me as a piece of writing which at once captures a distinctively Korean world-view and also develops a theme with transcendental appeal, as such it is especially suitable for

translation into an alien language. The unifying theme
is drawn from an old legend of Cheju Island about a
Utopian isle lying somewhere over the horizon of the
South Sea. The ocean, a common denominator which
beats the shores of every nation, has inspired great
literature from time immemorial. From the myth of
Atlantis to Melville's *Moby Dick*, from Coleridge's
Rime of the Ancient Mariner to Hemingway's *The Old
Man and the Sea*, people everywhere have from ancient
times been reduced to sighs and wondrous insignifi-
cance in the face of the immense and eternal waves of
the sea. *Iyǒ Island* is about these feelings of awe and it
is about the imagination of childhood. The universality
of the sea's fearful grace and of the struggle against the
loss of childhood's dream will resonate across space and
time through this translation, for those emotions are
surely the basis for a kind of universal grammar of the
soul.

Being a peninsular people, we Koreans have always
had an odd sort of ambivalence toward the sea: it feeds
us even as it threatens our lives. *Iyǒ Island* strives to
depict this blend of respect and terror, and to explore
the ways that these same emotions are evoked not only
by the impersonal majesty of the ocean, but by the impersonality of other unknowable forces, of war, or ab-
surd suffering, of human vulnerability. The artist
retreats inside the mind of a child to regain a precious
sort of credulousness that experience has tarnished.
Perhaps *Iyǒ Island* is an effort at recovering the
imagination of childlike conspiracies of optimism,
against all the forces that have driven the Korean people into a "Modern" attitude of resigned materialism.
The reader must judge for himself the extent to which

this novella succeeds in laying bare the profile of well-tempered illusion that serves to shield all of us, Korean and Occidental, from the harshness of life on the sea of impersonality.

To translate this work has been a far from easy labor, and experience has revealed that one cannot really hope to preserve the music of the Korean text, only to convey its gestural essence. English is relatively impoverished when it comes to words for describing affective tonalities, however I trust that I have not distorted too many passages beyond recognition. In a few instances it proved unavoidable to retain Korean words, but I believe the context adequately informs those occasions. Professor Chung's text displays the virtues of concise sentence structure and freedom from the tendency to parade a large vocabulary, hence the work should be accessible to readers at all levels and not merely intellectuals. I hope that *Iyŏ Island* transports its readers into the world of Korean imagination and leaves them with a curiosity to learn more about The Land of the Morning Calm.

Chun Kyung-ja

Iyŏ Island is not an island on any map, but a
paradise residing in the hearts of the fishermen of
Cheju Island.

Flotsam

My recollection begins with memories set in the rye
field back of our village, a village of only a few dozen
households, and of happenings on the trail beyond the
rye field. But it was not the trail and the rye field that
kept those memories alive, it was the seascape visible
from the hill that animated them. The sea contains
everything. All, therefore, that floats within my heart
is the sea, nothing more. Just as my memories surge
lively through the depths of the sea, so do the hopes
and passions of the sea flow back alive in my pulse. For
me, the sea has become eternity.

Now I seldom dwell on these things, but it was
otherwise through those six years of military service.
Whenever I had a free mo nent, such images would,
most unexpectedly, flash through my mind like lightning. Village, hills, rye fields, trails, always portents of
our hopes and dreams, never appeared in that lightning. The billowing sea alone inhabited those moments
of lightning. During my military life, which was a con-
catenation of rigors and ennui, the most pleasant thing
to do was to remember, immersed in towering waves
and scattering foam.

A spine of a hill, severed by some mishap, happened
to serve as a breakwall, and no one knew just when the
village of less than forty households had begun to grow
up behind it. Soon-Bok, Sang-Woon and I were the

same age, all born on the same day and year in that village. Identical age being a providential bond, we became the closest friends, enduring fights and jealousy. Discharged from the army, I returned home to find out that Sang-Woon had been killed on the Eastern front on one of those days I spent cherishing old memories in the army barracks. Although Sang-Woon's death in battle was the saddest event the rest of us had ever experienced, his loss left no unbearable sorrow or acute pain with me — perhaps, because memories of our happy youth remain much more vivid than the fact of his death.

Until we came to know the place called "school", our playground was always the boat and the sea. In the beginning, we could only manage to plunge in and out of the sea like frogs, but we took no satisfaction in that. We loved to go down to the bottom, like sea divers, to see who would be the first to land pebbles or clams. But as our tiny limbs grew more resilient, the swimming race from one end to the other of the hill became the high point of our days. We struggled with all our might, but the result was always a dead heat. We three were like that. Then, at last, we embarked on a new adventure.

It was one afternoon when a chilly wind was flailing the side of the boat. I don't recall which of us, right after lunch, was first to get on the boat, or who it was that first hit upon the idea. It is not even clear how the boat could have been standing there ready to sail at that time of day. What I still remember for certain is that together the three of us launched the boat and put out to sea. The moment we raised anchor we were seized by an indescribable anxiety, yet once the anxiety subsided we were swept along by an overwhelming power which allowed no soul to stand between us, and which relentlessly drove us to commit the dead.

We had never, up to then, been taught how to set a sail or row a boat. Still, we were confident we had both the skill and the strength to perform these tasks. Once the sail was set before the wind, the boat moved much faster than we had expected. By then all our initial anxiety had completely disappeared. It was then that we heard the shouts. At first, I pretended, like Sang-Woon and Soon-Bok, that I heard nothing, but at the second shout I couldn't help but turn my head.

"Young-Keun!"
The voice was calling me. I turned my head, holding the halyard.

"Pretend you didn't hear it."
Sang-Woon and Soon-Bok simultaneously stopped me. I dropped my head in spite of myself. Though I hung my head down, I could never erase from my mind what I saw at that moment. It looked like the whole village had rushed out on the shore, and I can still see my mother waving her hands wildly, calling for me to turn the boat back.

"If you want to go back, swim."
Those were the Sang-Woon's words. I couldn't stand it.

"Who said I wanted to go back?" I retorted, but it didn't help me feel any better inside.

My mother's face at first kept emerging with the clamorous shouts of the villagers from beneath the waves, but soon neither was seen or heard. Then new anxiety, like a thin layer of fog, quietly began building as the chilly wind breathed on my neck.

The seagulls cried, circling overhead. The three of us peered up and shouted. We were brought up on the shore, but never had we felt so good, so completely free from worry. The seagulls looked as if they were about to light atop the mast, but then, for no apparent reason, they flew off towards the horizon. It seemed they had volunteered to guide us, their new acquaintances, out to sea.

The wind was cold, but the sea wasn't very high. With the halyard still in my hand, I looked about absent-mindedly. Such mundane things as the shoreline were now far off, flickering hazily.

Soon-Bok and Sang-Woon were putting all their weight into the fluttering sail, which seemed about to be blown away at any moment. Over the horizon in the far distance, the clouds hanging beneath the sun looked especially beautiful, filled with dreams and mysteries. Even now, I remember every single, minute detail of the scene on that day.

From that point on, the color of the advancing waves differed entirely from that of the retreating ones. For the first time in my life, I could understand why my father always returned home after dark whenever he was out on the sea. It was impossible to tell whether the sea was reflecting the color of the sky or the other way around, or whether I was in a boat on the sea or was actually floating on top of the clouds. But then I came back to my senses at the boisterous laughter from Sang-Woon and Soon-Bok beside me.

"It's not just to catch miserable little fish like "jari" that our fathers bring their boats out here on the sea." Sang-Woon said. Soon-Bok, by then fatherless, remained silent. I agreed with Sang-Woon. Nobody, I thought, needs to sail all the way out to sea for some lousy *jari*.

"Let's try to find it."

There was a certain magic in Sang-Woon's voice. I felt an uncanny sense as my heart pounded away.

"If we can reach the spot where those clouds are gathered, it'll be there."

Sang-Woon smiled and nodded understandingly. What could it be that we were trying to find...?

We exchanged such remarks, but never once did any of us mention what it was we were searching for. It was something which to this day has not been revealed, and now that Sang-Woon had died in action, it had to remain forever a mysterious secret among us. Possibly, it was because of this same mysterious dream that Soon-Bok and I were once more aboard a boat and bound for the sea.

While serving my military duties, despite the hardships I had to face, I was always happy at those moments when I was revisited by these dreams. Although I knew that they would never be fulfilled, it's no exaggeration to say that I was incessantly regurgitating those dreams throughout my military life.

That seawater is just blue is an ignorant conception to people brought up by the sea. Like a fence erected by a stingy landlord to mark part of a field as his own property, there are similar kinds of fences to be found on the sea. A white streak of water marking a boundary line known as "nori", is the very same thing. It is a small wall made by colliding waves. The color of water within a *nori* and without is utterly different. Like a brilliant rainbow hung over the village beyond the hill

after a shower, the far side of a *nori* looked like a piece
of silk embroidered in a whole spectrum of colors.
Sang-Woon, Soon-Bok and I were each totally absorbed in that fantastic spectacle, all three of us grasping
the halyard.

How we had wandered the paths across the rye
fields and through the forest until our shirts were
drenched, trying to catch the rainbow! On those days,
our hands bled from the thorns and our legs would be
ragged out from sheer fatigue. Our dream never mate-
rialized, yet the same quest was repeated over and over
again.

It was on that particular day that I finally realized
that the grown-ups placed their hopes in the sea with
its rainbow-colored *nori*, just as our dream was confined in the rainbow, nowhere else.

What sent us into ecstasy, oblivious of all troubles,
might have been the very idea of a new discovery. The
sea was gradually turning its hue as the sky changed.
Like a radiant rainbow slowly slipping behind a cluster
of clouds, the bright color of the sea's *nori* was bit by
bit losing its color in the bosom of the cooling water.
The wind made us shiver. A new sense of uneasiness
replaced the ecstasy.

How aimlessly we wandered, blundering into cul-
de-sacs, when we searched for the rainbow! But then
we were never bewildered, nor did we ever feel any
uneasiness. Each time we would run up onto the high
hill, and by looking down at the sea below we could
easily find our way downwards.

The sea was growing darker. We were lost, no way
back to the shore. We regretted in vain that we hadn't
left any marks by which we could return home. The

three of us sat side by side under the sail. We were
trembling from cold and worry. We expected a
miracle, for we had unexpectedly discovered the
grown-ups' secret, but it was merely a vague hope.

"Look, there's a star!"
Soon-Bok blurted out. Still leaning my back against the
mast, I raised my head. The sound of his shout made
me completely forget my hunger. The stars we were
used to seeing from the forest or from the hilltop had
been far away from us, but now they were ever so
close. They looked like jewels mounted on the lid of a
container called "sea". It seemed as though we could
just pull down the streams of the Milky Way from
overhead and slip them into our pockets. Our lost
hopes and multiplying worries all disappeared at the
sound of Soon-Bok's shout.

"That's the North Star."

"Right. And that one is the Great Bear."

We had turned the boom by pulling the rope, but
the boat still didn't move much. Perhaps, the wind had
also dropped off to sleep in the darkness. We took turns
rowing. The Milky Way was flowing endlessly above
our heads. It seemed like our boat was no longer on the
sea but we were rowing on through the Milky Way.
Even though there was no strength left in our arms as
we rowed, as long as the stars shone above us we felt no
anxiety at all. The position of the stars before our eyes
seemed at once close and distant. No matter how long
we rowed in turn, the place we were aiming for was
nowhere to be seen.

The starlight was getting dimmer. Fog, like bundled
up balls of cotton, passed us by, touching our cheeks.
Now we were too exhausted even to stretch our backs.

I dropped down with a thud. Like a stone plummeting straight to the bottom, I felt I was going all the way down to the bottom of the deep sea. I couldn't lift a finger. My whole body seemed to be stuck tightly between huge rocks. Had I then really sunk deep under the sea...?

Something cold was bearing down on my face. I thought it was a broad piece of seaweed. If it was seaweed, I vaguely thought, wouldn't it be edible...? When this idea dawned upon me, I could no longer resist the hunger. I've never resented my voracious appetite as much as I did at that moment. I tried to move my unmovable body. I could barely wriggle a little. But I had to stretch out my hands, which was impossible. Resignation comes easily at such moments. So I just started licking at the stuff over my face.

There was no way I wouldn't recognize the smell and taste of seaweed, which had become a part of my own essence. The more the salty fluid dripped into my throat, the hungrier I felt. I could sense that my stomach, though practically stuck to my spine, was still working. But no matter how hard I chewed the stuff, it wouldn't break off.

"Well, it's morning now."
The voice sounded odd, like an echo from afar. It was the sort of voice we three used as a signal whenever we got lost on our way to catch the rainbow. Just then I nearly lost one of my front teeth when the stuff over my face was suddenly snatched away. The instant it was taken away I felt an emptiness over my whole body. I was not submerged deep in the sea, and it wasn't a seaweed I was chewing on. When I collapsed, someone took down the sail to cover me, and that was

what I'd been licking and chewing.

Unlike the day before, the sea was silvery and heaving. As Sang-Woon and Soon-Bok pulled in the anchor, I raised the sail. We looked at each other. Their faces were chafed, and their lips blistered. Unaware of what I was doing, I licked my own lips with the tip of my tongue. They felt slimy. Then, for some reason, I felt my face burning red.

I couldn't bring myself to tell them I had mistaken the sail for seaweed and had been licking and chewing it. To say such a thing would have been to reveal my weakness to them. Our friendship was, needless to say, the best there ever was. All the same, we were always competing or fighting over something. It was probably that sense of competition that wouldn't allow my pride to own up to it.

Things being as they were, we had no choice but to go whichever way the wind took us. Anxiety grows, after all, worse in the darkness. The fatigue and hunger remained, but the mere fact that we could now see each other's faces was enough to greatly ease our worries. The sea had changed completely as it welcomed the new morning. It seemed that our boat had stayed on the same spot all night through, but then again it looked like we'd drifted off in an entirely different direction. The mysterious dream that had been beckoning to us, those clouds that engulfed the entire horizon, the *nori* which seemed anxious to declare its own property rights, all had disappeared. The sea beneath the morning sun was a universe of silver light.

I was, as a matter of fact, in the Marines, but I spent more time on land than at sea. That I was hospitalized was, of course, part of the reason, but even after the truce, opportunities to get aboard a ship were very few. Come to think of it, it happened when I was taking part in West Coast operations.

I was in a small launch. But our boat wasn't involved in an amphibious landing. Being only a lowly private, I was not informed of our boat's mission, still I could gather we were responsible for making some sort of secret rendezvous. I remember that the sea was rough that day, and to make it even worse the tide was just then coming in. But with an urgent mission in hand, we couldn't just sit and curse the rough waves and the tide.

I still don't know what happened — whether the boat was hit by a torpedo and blown up, or was simply washed over by a sudden wave.... At any rate, from then until I was discharged from the marine corps, I never again saw any of the faces of the other men who were with me on that boat that night.

From the instant I hit the water I was knocked unconscious. Whenever on board ship we always wore life jackets, so we would float to the surface. Besides, I was confident that I could get out of the worst towering waves. I never saw the boat again because I was swept away in the currents. I couldn't see anything about me, but that didn't scare me. In the midst of the whirlpools, the only thing that came into my thoughts was the time the three of us stole a boat and put out to sea. Our first adventure on that day remained deep in our hearts as a mysterious dream. Who knows, maybe the reason we all joined the Marines was to find some way to realize that mysterious dream.

Although the waves were high and the sky dark, passing through my head as I was swept away was a clear, bright image of hope. I don't even know how, or by whom I was rescued. When I recovered consciousness in the hospital, all I knew was that one of my legs had been shot through.

When the time came for injured soldiers to leave the hospital, it was usual for them to cluster together and talk of their survival as a miracle of some kind. But even after listening to their stories, I never thought of my own case as any miracle. Everything that happened on that day had become a part of history, the past, yet the mysterious dream I envisaged belonged to the future, not to any past. To have a dream, even in the depths of despair, is always precious. Drifting on the water, I had grasped that precious dream until I once again lost consciousness.

It had been a minor injury, but I've been lame ever since. I lost the freedom of using one leg because it was disarticulated. But my handicap didn't keep me off of ships. Once aboard I was capable of working as much as healthy men, but I wasn't given a single chance to return to sea until I took off my uniform for the last time. I believe a marine's pride lies in working on board ship. That I was forced to remain shorebound and to limp my way about was an unbearable humiliation to me.

Morning on the ocean was a majestic sight, and one entirely new to us. Yet for all the magnificence of the spectacle, it held no charm for us. We were so exhausted from hunger and fatigue that there was no strength left in us to enjoy the scene. Of the three of us, I suppose Sang-Woon was the most discerning and the wisest. Whether it was discernment or wisdom, it was Sang-Woon, at any rate, who brought us new hope when we were entombed in despair.

"Good! Look at this! With this, now, we can solve our problem." As he spoke, he was pulling something out from the boat's hold.

"Wow! We're saved now!"

Now it was Soon-Bok's turn to shout, and only then I realized what it was. It was a net. A net....

I too felt life stirring inside me. As the huge net was patched together with knots, a renewed uneasiness was woven deep in our hearts. Until then none of us had seen anything but basket nets. We hadn't the slightest idea how to handle the enormous net.

"What are we doing?"

Unable to answer my question, Sang-Woon kept fumbling with the net. I looked vacantly up at the sky as if expecting a miracle. The sky too had recovered its own color, and was now showering a serene blue down over our heads. At the time I was certain I was inhabiting a dream. I was in fact reliving the incidents of the previous day. Whatever had become of the seagulls that had guided us, circling overhead? I thought the most important task was to discover their where-abouts. After all, we became lost when we lost track of them. But the sound of gulls was missing in the open air. I had to give up all hope. It was stupid of me, I thought, to expect a miracle. I sat down listlessly. I was utterly shocked when I saw Sang-Woon and Soon-Bok cutting the net with a knife.

"What are you doing?"

I found my voice trembling.

"What do you mean?"

I couldn't reply. They stared at my face, but their hands kept on working. I could sense a slight anger in

their expressions. It wasn't my father's boat, he had
hired it from the owner. Same with the net. Sang-
Woon and Soon-Bok knew how important the net was.
I had never felt so keenly how desperately the life of
my family depended on that very net. My heart was
burdened by the heavy silence. Thanks to the sunlight,
I felt a warm breeze caressing my neck. My father's
face appeared a couple of times, and I shut my eyes
tight to erase the image.

"The net is sacred...."
In the silence my voice carried more weight than the
sound of the waves slapping the bow.

"The net is important, but now it is more important
for us to survive."
I was moved by those words.

"If we live, there'll be another net, but if we die, the
net will be lost, too."
To hear Soon-Bok say such words pained me in an odd
way. It seemed to me that it wasn't Soon-Bok speaking
but an adult on some other boat. The pain I felt was a
shame I couldn't hide. I blushed deeply with my eyes
closed. I tried to justify myself to them, but couldn't
find any words to relieve the shame I felt. I was always
so sure I could beat them at any contest, but now I saw
what an idiotic creature I really was in the face of im-
minent danger.

It took a long while to make little basket nets out of
the huge net. We could see a school of fish passing
under the boat. I knew they were *jari*. It seemed to me
that we must be now in the area where the villagers
came for their daily fishing. I entertained yet another
secret hope that if we stayed on the same spot long
enough we might be able to meet the fishermen from

our village.

"Those are *jari*, aren't they?"

I asked to reassure my own hope.

"Right."

Soon-Bok threw the net into the sea. The fully extended net fell smoothly through the layers of seawater. I was amazed at his skill, for none of us had ever done it before. He started to pull in the net. By the way it swayed in the waves the net looked heavy, like it might be full of fish. In the sunlight, it was blinding to watch the tiny fish jumping out through the net. By the time it was pulled in, there weren't many left inside. A few little fish were flipping wildly, trapped between the two sides, but they were the kind nobody would bother with if they saw them twitching on the beach, washed up by the tide.

We were already exhausted after only one try. But we couldn't give up. Meanwhile I was watching the horizon in the far distance, hoping to glimpse even a shadow of a fishing boat. But there was nothing in sight. Only then I realized why those who left home before dawn couldn't return until after twilight.

Judging by the school of *jari* swarming under the boat, the place must had been my father's fishing grounds, but having seen no sign of any boats we were undoubtedly fairly far away from the village.

The *jari* we caught with our basket nets didn't even fill up a half gallon wooden bowl. Our disappointment was growing with each attempt.

People are odd. Now that I had returned home from my military service, my thoughts would linger more on military life, but during my entire time in the service I filled my days reminiscing about incidents that occurred in my native place, that tiny fishing hamlet.

In our village, nothing was a worse omen or threat than the words "poor catch". While I was out on the boat, I realized that the words had a unique power over our villagers. There were plenty of fish right in front of our eyes, but that we could still pull in empty net after empty net meant a lack of skill in catching them. Whenever my father and the other men left the village with their nets, the very notion of going out to catch fish could suggest the accursed words, "poor catch". So, I thought that as long as a fisherman was out on a fishing boat, he should not think he was out there to "catch" fish, but to "scoop" them into his boat. That was a dream I had, and to me it seemed a dream to live by.

The first vessel I served on was an L.S.T. Filling the boat with fish in my dreams... heedless of what I would do with that many fish if I could bring back them to our tiny village, I would peer at the horizon, my mind swimming with such dreams.

Exhausted, we sat down with a handful of *jari* strewn before us. They were still flopping high and low. We scaled and gutted them and ate them raw after a rinsing in seawater. Having been raised on the shore, we had eaten plenty of raw abalone, sea-cucumber and octopus, but raw *jari* was something new to us. Unlike any other raw seafood, as we ate them we had to separate the tiny bones with the tips of our tongues.

The first one so whetted our appetite that we gobbled up the rest without even scaling them. The smaller ones were easier to stuff in our mouths whole. We had almost emptied the half gallon wooden container when suddenly I tasted a strong bitterness in my mouth. I had to throw up. But even after I had emptied my stomach, I still felt nauseated and the pain in the pit of my stomach was so bad I felt momentarily blinded. I couldn't hear anything, and sweat poured out on my nose and my back. Never before had I endured such an ordeal.

I was utterly ashamed, for Sang-Woon and Soon-Bok were sitting next to me, and they could see me in that wretched state. My shame was an awareness of my ridiculous weakness as well as sorrow. But what I next heard was not their snickers as they laughed at me, it was a sound that once more upset my barely settled stomach. In the end they threw up, too, just like me. Not only the *jari* but my intestines themselves were turning inside out and seemed about to come out. I could no longer stand it and dropped flat on the bottom of the boat. The only sound audible was retching coming from Sang-Woon and Soon-Bok. The pain inside was so excruciating, I couldn't even move my little finger.

I don't know how long I stayed collapsed in that state, but I finally awoke from severe thirst. Though my eyes were open, everything in sight looked shrouded in purple and brownish yellow, revolving in slow motion. But I knew what I just heard a moment before was unmistakably the sound of a steam whistle. Then I heard it again.

"Help!"

"Help!"

The sound of the steam whistle was followed by a shrieking outcry from Sang-Woon and Soon-Bok. God only knows how such energy came forth from my worn-out, prostrated body, but I sprang up at once. I was still very dizzy and could hardly keep my balance, but I tried to scream as loud as they. Although I put all my strength into my shouts, they only made a feeble buzz in my ears.

"Do you see a ship coming?"
I asked them, unable to see anything clearly.

"No, it went away, gone!"
I was barely up, and now I felt like collapsing again. I couldn't even lift up my head for a long while. I was all ears, but no steam whistle was to be heard, and not a glimpse of a ship to be seen.

Since then, through my military years and the rest of my life, never have I been in such utter despair as I was on that day. Even so, faint hope lingered that fishing boats from our village might appear. By then there was something even more important than seeing a boat that would rescue us. It was the thirst. No one but a ship-wrecked mariner could understand what suffering it can be to be surrounded by water, and not be able to drink a drop of it. It was worse than the hunger we had earlier experienced. It was useless to moisten your lips with your tongue. The sunlight which had felt warm and pleasant in the early morning was no longer bearable.

I heard Sang-Woon and Soon-Bok moaning from time to time. Until then I was the defeated one, I thought, the one who'd revealed his weakness, so I was determined never to utter a single moan no matter what happened. I had to bite my lips as hard as I could to keep the growing pain within from issuing in a sound.

What was happening...? My burning, parched throat gradually felt cool and relaxed. Even in my half-conscious state, I couldn't forget the pleasant sensation. I realized, only much later, that some salty and faintly sweet liquid was flowing down my throat. I was also aware of a sharp pain on my lips. Yet, compared to the thirst, this pain was nothing. Suddenly, our boat shook violently. Involuntarily, I grabbed the side of the boat and opened my eyes. There was a sudden surge, not anything like a big wave striking, but from a whale underneath the boat. I leapt up and emitted a scream.

A ship, passing by us without blowing a whistle, seemed to slow down at my outcry. Again, I waved and shouted.

"Help!"

Soon-Bok and Sang-Woon, who had been prostrate until that moment, were now both up and shouting with me. The ship ignored our shouts and sailed on for a while before it turned around.

A moment of great sorrow turning into joy... the deep emotion I felt then still lives in my heart.

It was after dark when I woke up. The sleep helped me forget the hunger and the fatigue. My lips were swollen so badly I could hardly speak.

"Go outside and see. You'll find your friends there." The captain said gloomily without looking at me. He was staring outside with his hand on the hatch. I tried to look at his face, but only the tip of his pug nose was visible.

I went out. Darkness reigned over the sea, and the stars were shining like the night before. I saw Sang-Woon and Soon-Bok sitting outside. When I walked up to them, they didn't say a word. A stranger was squatting next to them, and another standing nearby. They were obviously among the ship's crew.

"Did you sleep enough?"
The man who was standing spoke to me. I hesitated for a moment. I knew he meant well, but wasn't sure how to respond. To avoid awkwardness, I changed the subject.
"Where is this ship bound now?"
"By the way, where are we now, sir?"
I wasn't the only curious one, Soon-Bok asked a question, too.
"What are you going to do if you know our location or the destination of this ship?"
It was quite unexpected. I merely had asked a question, and couldn't understand why he was so irritated about it. The guy who got upset at us walked off towards the captain's cabin, whistling. It was a whistle like the one a young fellow from Seoul, who stayed with the owner of my father's boat, used to do as he strolled along the beach alone. Somehow, I was more disturbed by the awkwardness of the situation than by the treatment given to my unwelcome question.
Soon-Bok, his head hanging, was deep in thought. Sang-Woon was, as was his way, busy trying to figure out our location from the stars. The ship picked up speed, cutting through the waves in the darkness and heavy silence.
"You're anxious to know, aren't you?"
Compared to the fellow who had just walked off toward the captain's cabin, the voice of this man was extremely gentle.
"We're now on the South Sea. If we safely finish our business tonight, we can have you back home by noon tomorrow."
He paused, glanced at us, then looked at the sea for a

while before continuing,

"But you must keep silent from now on, no matter what happens."

Although his voice was low, the tone was quite oppressive. What could their business be that had to be done safely...? I tried to figure it out, but couldn't come up with anything that even remotely fit in the picture. I just wished for them to safely accomplish their business, and prayed that we could be home by tomorrow.

"Sir, what kind of ship is this?"

Sang-Woon asked. The man didn't reply for a long while. We sensed he was reluctant to tell us.

"With a speedy ship like this, why don't you use it for catching fish instead of carrying cargo?"

Soon-Bok asked, and that was exactly what I had been wondering myself. But the man just smiled at our curiosity.

Judging by the deepening chill of the wind, it must have been quite late at night. The stars had become much livelier and sharper. But at sea one never knew what might happen.

"Sir, how do you know which way to go when you are on a wide sea?"

Sang-Woon asked the question which we all had been curious to know.

"The ship's course is plotted from a marine chart, but we can usually recognize directions from the experience of having been at sea for years."

We didn't completely understand his answer. A fog began to set in, gradually occluding our surroundings.

"Fog coming. Looks like the Dragon God is astir. Now, you be quiet, else the Dragon God will pull you into the water."

I felt a cold sweat running down my back, and kept still. Sang-Woon and Soon-Bok also seemed to be holding their breath. To us, the Dragon God, with his magic powers, was a fearful being. As we grew up, we had become accustomed to the rituals for the Dragon God, held twice a year, once in the Spring and again in the Autumn.

The ship suddenly slowed, and we heard a strange thumping noise coming from the bottom. We were most worried that something had gone wrong with the ship, but nobody dared to speak. The light in the captain's cabin was extinguished. The sailor who had been staying with us looked to the bridge. Now they stopped the engine completely. The heavy fog swept us and the whole ship into a dread. Then we were sure we heard an engine running in the distance that sounded like our engine. The shadow of the sailor standing beside us wavered. He ran up to the bridge. For some reason the sight of his back made me anxious. The sound of opening and closing the hatch door was loud in the darkness, and then everything fell back to silence. I tried to look at Soon-Bok and Sang-Woon, but their faces were so thickly shrouded in fog I couldn't make them out. The starlight overhead was no longer visible.

"Something broken down?"

I said to myself, aloud.

"No, I don't think so."

Soon-Bok answered. If nothing was out of order, what was going on then? I wanted to ask Soon-Bok something else, but I couldn't think very clearly.

"Right. Nothing wrong, they've just turned the engine off."

Sang-Woon also sounded vaguely worried. At that instant someone walked out of the captain's cabin and came towards us.

"Now, kids, be quiet."

It was the young fellow who earlier had been upset with us and left.

"You three, come this way."

We did as told. The place we entered was the galley. Although it was called a galley, it was no more than a corner beneath a porthole. Once we were down there, the young fellow closed the hatch from above.

Unaware what was going on, we were kept penned up in the box-like galley, trembling with fear. Down there, we noticed for the first time how badly the ship was rolling, which wasn't so noticeable out on the deck. After they had killed the engine, the ship seemed to be rocking along with the waves.

Hurried footsteps were audible from above. We had not the faintest idea why they were running about after they locked us up. When the sound of the footsteps died down, I opened the hatch slightly by pushing it with my head, seeking some clue to the mystery. Though it could not be seen, I could feel the fog cascading down. At that very moment the ship shook so abruptly that I dropped down onto my seat. After a while longer we at last understood the nature of the rocking. They were dropping anchor there.

Did they drop anchor because the sudden, dense fog prevented them from moving any further? But then, why did they have to shut us up, and what of the steam whistle that sounded in the distance as soon as they killed the engine? There was no one willing to give any definite answers to my many questions. Feeling something big or small without being able to see it, can instill fear. Something heavy touched the ship.

"What could it be?"

"Something is hitting the ship, isn't it?"

Quickly I answered Sang-Woon's question, and strained to listen outside.

"It was a coast guard cutter, wasn't it?"

"Yes, we were nearly caught."

The fellow who had thrown us down asked the question, and an unfamiliar voice answered him. The words "coast guard cutter" stirred a strange curiosity in me.

"Think we'll be all right?"

"Guess so."

Their brief conversation made me shudder. What reason did they have to avoid a coast guard cutter? As this question popped into my mind, all my hopes evaporated, and I was again depressed. We thought we'd been rescued, but in fact we were trapped in a tiger's mouth. Even the gentle sailor's promise of a safe return home by tomorrow seemed a mere lie. His kindness might have been deliberately feigned to calm us down. Seeing how cautious the crew is evading the coast guard cutter, anyone could tell that the ship was no ordinary one.

The nature of the ship made me even more fearful. My mind was filled with pirate ships from story books I had read.

"Now, hurry and unload the cargo."

"Everything ready?"

"You needn't worry about it."

They were holding hooded lamps that didn't shed light very far. Occasionally, the light seeped in

through the crack in the hatch cover I made by
pushing it a little with my head. At those moments, the
faces of Sang-Woon and Soon-Bok were dimly visible,
as in a dream.

"What kind of boat is that?"

"We found it on the way."

"Is it good enough to use?"

"I don't know."

I felt dizzy. We were unquestionably lost, and now
it was obvious that our boat was about to be lost, too.
No longer able to contain my dread, I whispered to
Soon-Bok, who was next to me.

"What can we do?"

"This is no time to worry about the boat."

Soon-Bok, too, must have been listening carefully to
their conversation.

"If we misstep now, we'll blow the whole thing.
We're like birds in a net, now. Got to wait and see."

As we exchanged these words, they began unloading
the cargo. I didn't think they had much, but it took
them quite a while to unload it. None of us knew the
nature of the cargo, or the identity or destination of the
ship. The only thing still clear in my memory is that
the ship sailed at full throttle before and after
unloading in darkness beneath the dense veil of fog.
We didn't see the whole operation, because the
unloading took a long time and we fell asleep in the
meantime.

We went back on deck after they woke us. The morning and night on the sea had left no trace, and the sea
was as clear and bright as ever. My foremost concern
was our boat. The moment we reached the deck, I
looked for it without attracting anyone's attention.

Unexpectedly enough, the boat, which I imagined was gone, was hanging out there. It was almost submerged underwater, but that it was still there was a miracle to me.

The fog lifted for a while and then descended again. Unlike the previous night, the ship was now constantly blasting its steam whistle. It was sailing at full speed, but then made a wide turn and gradually slowed down. The captain said something to us, but we couldn't make out what he was saying.

"You said your place is where the stepping stone is, didn't you?"

"Yes."

"Your village is over there."

But the spot indicated by the sailor was invisible in the dense fog. The ship stopped. We had to get off the ship and on to our own boat as ordered. We were told that our village was dead ahead of us, but we couldn't believe it. The front window was wide open, and the captain said he wished he could take us all the way to our village but the draft was too shallow for his ship to enter. After what he told us, we couldn't ask any more of him. I was the first to pick up an oar. Just then I got a clear look at the captain's face as well as the faces of the other two sailors.

When their ship sailed off at full speed, our boat was greatly rocked by the wake. We waved until their faces vanished from sight.

The pirate ship enigma left us with a million questions which were not solved until many years afterwards, after I joined the Marines. It was the first time I was aboard ship. There was one officer who looked quite out of place. It wasn't just his age, but his crooked frame made him appear anything but a navy officer. He was the chief engineer. Everyone, officers as well as sailors, called him "uncle".

It took a long time before I could place him in my memory. Then, I realized he was unmistakably the fellow who had gotten upset at us for no good reason. I couldn't believe my own eyes when I saw that time had transformed that irritable man into such a calm, gentle person. I could never forget those faces I had scrutinized so closely as we moved to our boat.

As soon as I finished my meal at the privates' mess, I went outside to wait for him. As expected, having dined in the officers' mess, he came out towards where I was waiting. Somehow, neither the military cap nor the uniform was becoming on him.

"Uncle!"

Addressed in that manner by an unknown sailor, he looked more puzzled than angered.

"Do you remember the incident on the South Sea?"

"The South Sea?"

Quietly he repeated the question, and then blushed. From his red face, I grew confident that he was the man.

"It's now a long forgotten story, but...."

As if straining to recall ancient history, he gazed at me with narrowed eyes. I didn't wish to remind him of the incident by telling him the story myself. Instead, I lifted my face, hoping he would be able to locate the old, lost incident in his memories. But he didn't seem to be able to connect a handsome sailor with the face of the young boy, adrift and nearly dead, who had crossed his path at one point years before.

"I mean the three boys you rescued."

Only then he seemed to gather a hazy picture. He stared at my face for a long time, then finally shouted,

"Sure! Of course, I remember! Indeed, I do!"

He was a bit excited.

"So, you were able to return to your village that day, weren't you?"

I nodded lightly, and looked over the railing at the sea. A sea bird that had been hovering over the waves at that touching moment flew up and began circling above us.

"That day, too, we were visited by a bird like that one."

There arose in my heart an inexplicable blend of anxiety and hope similar to what I had felt on that morning. The bird soon disappeared, but we remained sitting as before.

"When did you begin sailing, uncle?"

"Right after the Korean War...."

An anguished look came over his face.

"What a strange coincidence. So, you are one of the boys we took aboard that ship?"

He seemed to be fumbling through his own memory.

"What happened to the other men who were with you on that ship?"

He silently held his chin in his hands, and was absorbed in deep thought.

"Now it's all like a dream."

Indeed, the past was like a dream. Yet, I could never completely free myself from the attractions of those haunting dreams. It was to realize those dreams that I went to sea again later, after discharge from the military.

That mysterious dream — that indelible image,

never to be erased. In a way, it had become an inseparable part of me.

"You knew then what our ship was doing, didn't you?"

"I wasn't quite sure, but I had an idea."

"Being 'not quite sure' is always best."
He almost smiled, but then as if something had just occurred to him, his face darkened. We remained sitting there, immersed in nostalgia, oblivious of life's complexities.

"After that, we did the same thing a few more times. We did it for the money. After all, it's money that makes the world go round, and we needed some."
He cocked his hat, pushing one side up off his head. That was when I saw a big scar on his forehead that I hadn't noticed before.

"Do you remember seeing this scar on my face before?"
I shook my head. Although that morning I had seen his face clearly, no such memory had stayed with me.

"If I've held on to anything, it's this scar."
A sailor from the engine room walked up and saluted him. He nodded. He listened to the private's report and nodded. Then he stayed for a while longer before getting up. I also rose after him.

"Some other time we'll talk more. Anyway, this scar is all there is left for me. The money I sought, the friends I trusted... they're all gone, this scar is the only thing left behind...."
His unfinished sentence quavered lightly with a ring of sorrow.

"It's nice to run into an old friend. Since we're on the same ship, we'll see each other often enough. Next time

I'll talk in more detail. It was nice to see you. Today,
I've got things to do...."

I saluted his back as he spun around, and watched him
walk away.

After that day, though we were on the same ship, I
never had a chance to sit down with him to hear his
promised tale. Then I received orders for a different
operation which forced me to change ships. I never
saw him again while I was in the Marine Corps. The
origin of his scar and why he lost the money and
friends remained a mystery. I racked my brain attempting to answer those questions on my own. They had
piled up some cash by smuggling, but there was an in-
evitable dispute in dividing the shares, followed by a
betrayal, then the scar.... I've often mused like a detec-
tive about solving the conundrum, but never came up
with any clear, definite conclusion.

Although we didn't have complete faith in them
when they told us our own village with its stepping
stone was ahead of us, after they disappeared from
sight, we rowed in that direction. The heavy fog began
to move away quickly. We stared into the fog as if trying to discover something inside it. Nothing. Again we
strained our ears. We were sure we heard something,
but then only the wind would pass by us. I almost
dropped the oar. Through a crack in the fog, as it
drifted away like smoke, I saw a hill. It was the hill
which served as a jetty for our village. On all three of
our faces, there appeared more apprehension than
relief.

I handed the oar over to Soon-Bok. For some reason
I felt disheartened and couldn't row any longer. Soon-
Bok wasn't very brisk with his rowing, either. The anx-

iety of returning home may have been greater than the joy.

It was odd that the whole village was so still on such an occasion. Contrary to our wish for cover beneath the fog, it suddenly cleared up. The shore was now within reach. Yet there was not a soul on the street by the pier, and nobody on the hillside. The entire place seemed completely changed. The spirit of hope we had two days before as we sailed away turned into foam melting into the sand on the shore.

Having pulled the boat aground, we stood there a long time, enveloped in apprehension. We felt like empty shells washed up by the waves. The anxiety oppressing us was nothing like what we had felt while adrift, nor was it anything like the sorrow we experienced whenever we were scolded at home.

We trudged up the hill in silence, and when we reached the fork in the road, each took his own way. Up to then we hadn't run into anyone. I approached my house and hesitated. Then I saw my mother run out with bare feet and our dog John following her. Someone must have told her I was coming. John was the first to greet me, jumping all over me. That was how John always said hello whenever I came home. I loved John dearly, so much as to be almost bothersome to him. But on that day, I found his love unbearable. I pushed him away a couple of times, and finally broke into tears. I didn't know why, but I was overwhelmed by sorrow and wept loudly. I was still crying when my mother came up to me. She shooed John away and held my hands.

"Oh, dear, where have you been? I thought you were surely drowned. Oh, I'm so glad you're back, so very glad...."

I had never known my mother's voice so gentle as that moment. She didn't cry like me, but she wiped tears from her eyes.

The news of our return spread at once throughout the village, turning the whole place inside out. The more people made a row over of our return, somehow the more embarrassed I felt to go out.

It was only later that we learned that the day after our disappearance, not a single fishing boat in the village went out fishing for *jari*. Instead, all the boats were used to search for us. On the day we returned, too, they all had left at dawn to scour Cheong San Do Sea. My father was on one of the boats, so he wasn't home when I came. They didn't return until late that night, but the villagers, including my mother, didn't seem too concerned about their absence.

The episode which had stirred up the whole village gradually died down as time went by. But among our age group, it never ceased to be a great subject of talk. Not only in our school, but also in a school two miles away, it was talked about. Just as we were lured to our first adventure by dreams and hopes that had long been stirring in our hearts, the other boys asked us questions to fulfill their own dreams. In truth, we didn't really know anything that would enable us to answer their questions with anything worth listening to. But it wasn't right to lie to them just to satisfy them. Though we had little to share with the other boys, there was still secrets which only the three of us knew — the place for catching *jari*, the place with a mysterious dream over the horizon and the ship that had brought us back home.

Sometimes when Sang-Woon, Soon-Bok and I were in the same group assigned to do cleaning chores after school, we would collect all our knowledge about geography, draw a map on the blackboard with our teacher's leftover chalk, and do our best to figure out the approximate spot where we had been drifting. We never succeeded in confirming the place.

We strove so eagerly to locate the place not just to satisfy curiosity. Although not a word about it was ever exchanged among the three of us, it was mutually understood that we were conferring not about a past adventure that had failed, but to lay plans for a new adventure which, without a doubt, would end successfully.

A Boat Song

It was the sea that took away all my hopes and remembrances of the old days. The sea abandoned me, but I haven't forsaken it yet. To be cast away was miserable, but more miserable than abandonment itself was the inability to withdraw even after being abandoned.

That was exactly my situation at that time. The sea abandoned me but I was still clinging to it, making my life at sea. The stepping stone on the smoothly sloping hill was bombed into oblivion during the war. But, our village was still known as "Stepping Stone Valley" or "Rock Village".

Now the scars had become less prominent, but after I returned home, the traces of war were everywhere vivid—the shattered rock, the demolished houses, the people flocking together for refuge, and so on. All those sad marks were slowly fading away. They disappeared like the red spots of measles on a child's face disappear as the fever subsides. Almost everything was reconstructed in its old form, but neither the disintegrated rock nor my heart could ever be restored to their former condition.

Everyone in the village had asked me to work on their boat, but I firmly declined. Not that I had any special reason, I just lacked the will to go that path. In fact, were I deprived of the pleasure of going to sea alone, I might have lost the thrill of life at sea altogether.

There was another, more complex, reason why I couldn't desert the sea even after it deserted me. Whenever I rowed out to sea, the happiness of that day long ago always came back alive within me—the uncertainty and the excitement. Each time I had to cast my eyes to the horizon in order to subdue my inflamed emotions. Still, the excitement and anxiety were not such as to lead me to repeat the old adventure. What I was searching for was the Ocean's lost regions. Even if I succeeded in finding the place again, the old sorrow and the old memories would certainly not turn into joy.

Why, then, did I persist in attempts to discover the place? It never left my mind, yet not even once did I find it... the place with the white *nori* resembling some landlord's boundary mark, pregnant with dreams of uncanny clouds, the place that beckoned us with its blue waves.... That was where our dreams and desires led. But they turned out to be no more than airy foam. I don't mean it saddened me. What was sad was our dream that never came true.

The weather was unusually fine for the season. The afternoon sunlight was so warm it almost made you doze off. In winter, such a day comes but once or twice a year. When I arrived there, my heart began to race for no good reason. Not just my heart, my face blushed any my limbs trembled. The white *nori* trailing its wake behind, the blue water line and the cumulus clouds... it seemed like the place we three little boys once passed by. Hurriedly, I dropped anchor and looked about. It wasn't that we left any sign there. The only guide was my own intuition.

Still, after looking around, I realized it wasn't the same place. I forgot to cast the net, and just sat there quietly for a long time. Where, then, could the mysterious waters be that still shone in my memory? They lingered in my mind, but were impossible to locate in reality. I deeply lamented my error. There had been a chance for me to rediscover the lost place. It was when I, as a marine, ran into the old chief engineer. I should have asked him at once where the place was. Now I didn't even know if he was among the living.

The boat was sliding through the waves. Only then I realized that I had forgotten to pull in the net. As always, it was hard to pull in the net alone. Though I was crippled, my leg was supposed to be completely healed. But every time I used it for any hard work, there was a throbbing ache. As I retrieved the net, I closed my eyes slowly—the only way to endure the pain.

By the feel of the net in my hands, I could tell there weren't many fish in it. Still, I couldn't let the net drop back in the water when I'd pulled it halfway out. As expected, the catch was negligible. Feeling no urge to try again. I sat there idly. It wasn't at all easy to catch fish by myself. Even so, I wanted no company when I went out to sea.

As the pain in my leg eased, one of my arms began to quiver. I tried not to think about Soon-Bok, but his face appeared before my eyes at such moments. Fish or no fish, if only he were there with me, I wouldn't have felt half as lonely. Now, that wish had been reduced to a dream of recapturing the past.

I had not the faintest inclination to cast the net again. But I wasn't ready to turn the boat around, either. Just then I entertained a vague wish that the boat would capsize. It wasn't at all likely that a boat would flip over on such calm seas, and I lacked the courage to jump into the water. It had occurred to me while alone that I would probably remain behind as the only survivor among the three of us, and I alone would be telling the melancholy tale of our first adventure.

At that time I had recently returned from the service. Just as the village and its natural features were changed, so had my own family. My mother had already passed away some time before, and my younger sister had gone away with an American soldier stationed nearby. My father was left alone in the house. To be honest, if I had known the unfortunate circumstances, I wouldn't have returned at all.

That I had had so few contacts with my home was partly because I had been in the hospital and partly because it was on a remote island well out into the South Sea. At first, I resented being back in that place. But once I set foot there, I couldn't turn my back on it, and it was not just because of my old father, either.

From then on, Soon-Bok and I went out fishing on the same boat. Our family wasn't the only one in the village that had suffered misfortunes. It is pointless to recite the story of each and every household, since their travails were not matters of pride. The instances of our three families should suffice. I've already spoken of Sang-Woon and myself, and Soon-Bok was in a similar situation. By the time I came back home, Soon-Bok was practically leading his entire life on a boat, seldom stepping onto land. I could readily comprehend his strange behavior without inquiring into motives. All the same it struck me as odd that he never left the village, even when he led his life beyond its confines.

I rowed and Soon-Bok worked the sail. Naturally, we put out to sea to catch *jari*. But Soon-Bok looked at the village from the boat in a different way than he gazed at the seaward horizon. His eyes glancing at the hills, the rye fields and the paths stretching beyond the fields across the land of our dreams and memories were no longer the same eyes of the child who followed the rainbow. Now these eyes cast looks full of sorrow and anguish on the village, and only when turned to the open horizon would they shine once more with thirst for the unknown.

Once we were out at sea, Soon-Bok usually handed the boom line over to me, and he would take the oars himself. Oars in hand, his eyes shone brightly, and his lips trembled. As he rowed, a boat song naturally came flowing from his mouth. Nobody had taught it to him, it was something gradually absorbed, like a seaman gradually gets accustomed to the sea breeze. But his boat song had a peculiar tone. Rope in hand and eyes closed, an exhilaration coursed through my heart which seemed to bear us onward to the mysterious region of dreams and hopes, to the place we once searched for. Soon-Bok didn't appear to be a man who ventured so far into the sea merely to catch *jari*.

Sometimes when he looked too tense, I couldn't help feeling worried about him. What was it that was mirrored in his brilliant eyes? What was it that he was seeking in such an ecstatic state? As far as I knew, the object of his search was nothing on the sea. What he was picturing in his mind didn't seem to be our long lost region. More precious visions than that beckoned not from the sea, but from some unknown land.

Although I only learned of it after my return, shrapnel from a bombshell had killed Soon-Bok's mother during the war. Among the three of us of identical age, he was the first to marry, supposedly because he was the only child of a single mother. Perhaps that was why he never could bring himself to leave the place for good, though he had abandoned his house and was staying on his boat.

Soon-Bok's wife, I was told, left the village less than a year after he was drafted. I only heard about it after I left the military, and there were many different versions of the story. Some said she lived in Incheon where her own family had moved, others claimed they had seen her in a red light district somewhere in Seoul, and so on. None of them were particularly reliable. They were just rumors spread by gossip through the village.

The sea took everything away from me, and in the end it devoured Soon-Bok, too, the pillar of my soul. I wouldn't be able to proceed directly to telling of his death. I first have to describe our life together, then perhaps I can recall his death in a less tumultuous state of mind. At any rate, Soon-Bok no longer shares our lives on this side of the universe. It would be futile to pose any questions to him now... but what could he have been searching for in the sea? That alone remained as the riddle which ate away at my mind.

For eight months after I came home I lived with Soon-Bok. Why couldn't I have moved away with him to some other place? He and I were never apart except to sleep. Our boat was small, but it was a heavenly sanctuary for us. If we had gone straight to the hills where we once wandered in pursuit of the rainbow until our jackets turned damp, and if we had never again set foot on a boat, then we probably would have left the village once and for all. Then I might have escaped suffering today's tragedy all by myself. Such were my vain daydreams. Now that everything was over and done with, even to dream of such things meant yet another occasion for self-torture.

I had to cast the net again. While putting the net in order I suddenly stopped and strained my ears. The net trembled along with my hands, and my heart pounded violently. I dropped the net and stood up. The wind had died down, and the water was smooth and calm.

Ah, Iyŏ Island, Iyŏ Island!
Cumulus clouds o'er the sea
As a boat glides onwards.
Ah, Iyŏ Island!

What I heard was unquestionably a boat song, but when I peered about me, not a soul was in sight. And the song was already over. The silence of the ocean was

deafening. I slowly shut my eyes. It was the first verse
of the boat song Soon-Bok used to sing as he rowed.
The forgotten song floated back to my mind.

Ah, Iyŏ Island, Iyŏ Island!
You, my true love
Have you gone to Iyŏ Island?
Ah, Iyŏ Island!

Ah, Iyŏ Island, Iyŏ Island!
That boat yonder, sails unfurled,
Is she off to Iyŏ Island?
Ah, Iyŏ Island!

Those eyes.... When he sang, Soon-Bok's eyes shone
brightly. It wasn't only the image of those luminous
eyes, I also heard his deep, mournful voice and the
sound of his harsh breathing.

I had not the energy, courage or desire to cast the
net. Finally, I collapsed, burying my head between my
knees. Like towers of dark clouds that released no rain,
my eyes shed no tears as my heart was inundated with
indescribable sorrow.

Iyŏ Island... an island no one had ever visited, and
no one even knows where it lies. Yet, it was an island
boat men yearned for from time immemorial. The
origin of the song of Iyŏ Island was unknown, but to me
it seemed that dreams and adventures like our own
must have sustained our ancestors through their sor-
rowful and miserable lives.

Iyŏ Island was a mysterious land of dreams and
hopes, but it was a tragic land, as well, for none had
succeeded in grasping its promises. Why did Soon-Bok

imagine his wife, who had vanished without a trace,
on Iyŏ Island? Hope knows no bounds, and tragedy lies
in ambush in the far reaches of hope. Immersed in such
thoughts, abruptly I lifted my head.

Ah, Iyŏ Island, Iyŏ Island!
Cumulus clouds o'er the sea
As a boat glides onward.
Ah, Iyŏ Island!

The singing which had died down was heard once
more. I couldn't just sit there and listen. I turned the
boat in the direction from which the singing came. I
don't recall how long I pursued the sound. When the
color of the water started to alter, the sky would, as
always, hurry to meet the twilight. I remained unable
to find the singer of that song in that infinite sea. Only
the billowing waves were to be seen, not a single boat
from which the song could've issued. Who could be
singing that song?

It might as well have been an hallucination, no matter how hard I scanned about there was not even the
shadow of a boat. But I couldn't dismiss it as a mere illusion. I could identify no earthly reason for such an inexplicable phenomenon. Compelled to turn the boat
around without having found the singer, I felt a sor-
rowful gloom building like thickening fog in my heart.

I had no will to row. I stood absent-mindedly as the
twilight reflected on the water. A long forgotten
memory dimly resurfaced in my mind. I realized it was
anything but an old recollection, rather it was an
urgent matter I had to carry out at once. I grabbed the
oars with renewed vigor, and turned the boat out of its

lazy tidal drift toward shore.

I had to attend an Arts Festival at the village grammar school that evening. It wasn't that I'd received a personal invitation from the old principal himself, nor was it because I was expected to appear as an official representative of the Disabled Veterans' Association. I had to go because Soon-Bok's son, Kil-Nam, that morning had asked me to come to the festival without fail. I knew very well that Kil-Nam had for days been patiently waiting for that night. I also knew that the occasion meant something special to Kil-Nam, who had little to take pride in before his peers in the village. If not for this special plea from Kil-Nam, I probably wouldn't have given it a second thought.

It was getting dark. My mind was churning. Even the weak sound of waves slapping at the boat's hull sounded to me like clamourous excitement of the villagers, clustered to view the performance held in a classroom of the tiny grammar school. I wasn't really rowing. Sitting amidst the spectators, I was taken back to my grammar school days.

The Arts Festival

"How come you're so late?"
Father asked, but, distracted by other thoughts, I couldn't answer him and just mumbled.

"Well, it takes even longer on days you don't catch much, that's the way it is."
The old man, aged by the sea, answered his own question, puffing on his long pipe. The sweet smelling smoke somehow stimulated my hunger.

I left the net hanging out on the line and went into the room. I meant to change clothes, though the only other set of clothes I had was my Marine uniform. I didn't particularly like the uniform, but had no other choice. As I was changing in the dark, my father said,
"Kil-Nam has been in and out since early evening, looking for you."
"There's some performance at school tonight."
"I thought so. Looked like everyone in the village was headed there. If you knew it, you should have returned earlier."
I came back out of the room. Perhaps the weather was turning bad, for the night was unusually dark.
"Aren't you going to have a bite before you go?"
Father seemed greatly attentive to every single move I made. The hunger I felt a while before was no longer there. Besides, even if I hurried, I couldn't get there on time. I didn't feel much like eating, anyway.
"I'll eat when I come back."
Through the dimly lighted window the sound of father's coughing was audible. As he said everyone must have gone to the festival, because the village was awfully quiet and dark.
On the way up the hill, I chanced to look back. Only the gurgling of the waves broke the stillness of the village. I saw a twinkling light out in the waves. I watched it for a long time despite being in a rush.
"Who could it be?"
At first, I couldn't imagine who might be out casting nets at night beneath a lamp. Still, I fancied I could hear each kind word exchanged among them as they worked with the nets.
A moist, chilling breeze swept by, striking my cheeks

as if to urge me on. The light bobbing in the waves twinkled once more. The men on the boat were not who I'd imagined them to be, and the voices I thought I heard didn't belong to those unfamiliar faces I couldn't place. The shadows and the whispers had belonged to Sang-Woon, Soon-Bok and me.

We always wanted to have a secret refuge of our own. But, not even that bit of freedom was allowed to young boys like us. So, we used to meet at an empty boat agreed upon ahead of time. But we never again repeated the adventure of taking the boat out onto the wide open sea. That we never used the cloak of darkness to go out to sea wasn't because the darkness deprived us of our courage or adventurous spirits. The warm, little lamp we lit in the evenings where we gathered always slaked our thirst for wandering, somehow.

Again, the din of waves battering the shore could be heard. At the sound of the waves, I grew oblivious of my destination, and stood there reliving my past. No longer was I a crippled man standing on the hill, but a little boy sitting before a lamp. Wrapped up in pale worries, we forgot the tender whispers of the stars. No one appeared to unbind as from the night's anxieties. That night we solemnly vowed we would repeat our crime, bring Soon-Bok's mother to school, but we didn't know what we had done wrong, nor why our teacher intended to punish us.

The waves had caused the twinkling light to drift away. My thoughts stayed on unlit paths. Summer was anchovy season in our village. After school, pupils went directly home to help unload the anchovies from the boats, working until dark. Soon-Bok, Sang-Woon and I never cared for those duties, and we often shunned it on the pretext of having to stay late at school. Throughout the long summer afternoons, we would hang about the schoolgrounds after class was out. The only thing to do was to play games in the shade of the willow tree that stood at one end of the playground.

Our school was the largest building in the village, but it was only a one story wooden structure with four rooms, three used for classes, and one reserved for the teachers. The school was co-ed and covered grades one through six. Each classroom mixed students of two different years together. The bald principal had seemingly always been in charge of the fifth and sixth graders. A young male teacher, Yoo-Cheol Kim, taught the third and fourth graders, and a recently arrived young woman taught first and second graders.

The principal lived on the school property. His small, tin-roofed house stood beyond the playground. He had allotted himself a corner of the yard for a vegetable garden and was always busy at work on the garden as soon as the school day ended. Of course, his garden was smaller than the rye field on the hillside, but it had no slope, and I still remember how, from early spring through late autumn, it was always full of growing things. He didn't look like a principal at all once he took off his teaching suit and commenced dragging a manure pail around the garden, a straw hat slanting over his forehead. When he appeared, we would stop our game beneath the willow tree and smile as our eyes met.

The produce grown by the principal in his garden was often used in our science class. When the peppers in the principal's garden turned bright red, we knew it was the season for cicadas. By then the classroom doors were closed and we were almost the only ones on the playground.

We could see that the window of the teachers' room was still open. Bored with our games, we would lie in the shade using our bookbags as pillows. Those were the times we listened to the sound of organ. On the empty playground, with no apparatus for sports, lying down on our bookbags and listening to organ music became our newly discovered form of consolation.

Since the arrival of the female teacher, we often heard her playing the organ. The music she played was a sort we had never heard before. Though we didn't know the names of the different pieces, they raised our spirits somehow when we sprawled there in exhaustion. It wasn't only the sound of organ that reached our ears, we could also hear our teacher, Yoo-Cheol Kim, singing along with the organ. It was no small surprise for us; for we thought the National Anthem which he taught us to sing, was the only song Mr. Kim knew.

Sometimes we would walk up to the open window and sneak a look into the teachers' room. We were safe since the woman teacher faced the wall as she played the organ, and teacher Kim was absorbed in his singing. The new female teacher was always a marvel to us, and teacher Kim looked especially handsome on such moments. But our wonder lasted only for the first couple of times, and when it became a daily event, we soon lost interest. The three of us were the only ones who knew about it, since we usually hung around school until late.

There was another new discovery that helped us escape the choking boredom we encountered as days grew dark. We hid this new treasure in the bushes beside the outhouse behind the school building, for we knew the kids seldom went there to play. Our new discovery was actually nothing extraordinary. During the Dragon God Ceremony some of the villagers had slaughtered a pig. We never found out how he got it, but Sang-Woon managed to bring us the pig's bladder. The three of us took turns blowing it up, and it became our sole object of diversion and exercise. When the last kid on sweeping duty left school, we used to have a great time, throwing and kicking it around. One day, the kids on the sweeping duty wouldn't leave, like they'd decided to discover how we spent our time after school. We nonchalantly played our usual game on the playground, under the scalding sun. The game we played, called "*gonu*", was the sort of game that gets boring after a few times, even if you are playing with an arch rival. So, it was only natural for the other kids to grow bored, especially when they were only watching. Pretending to love the game, we were about to start all over when they gave up and left. As soon as they passed through the gate, we rushed to the back of the school building.

As I ran ahead of my friends, I suddenly halted. I looked back, and Sang-Woon and Soon-Bok also stopped heading toward the bushes for the ball and looked back at me. It was the new woman teacher, no mistake. At that moment, an odd question came to my mind. Do teachers go to the toilet, too? Even lady teachers? Until that instant, I always assumed that the principal and other teachers would never go to the outhouse like us to pee or crap. Such things were possible for our parents, but never for teachers. The principal and the teachers up to then were like gods to me. My shock and curiosity were really immense. Our exchange of glances was a kind of mutual pact that we should satisfy our curiosity.

We went around to the back of the outhouse. The back window was open, but it was too high for us to peek in. Sang-Woon bent over, and Soon-Bok got on top of his back. I climbed up on their backs and stood up. The teacher was in a sitting position, and I was sure I heard some kind of noise.

Whether Sang-Woon or Soon-Bok moved, or I made a false step from nervousness, no one knew. Anyway, I cried out as I fell to the ground. At that instant, I met with a fierce stare from the woman teacher. I could only remember her dagger-sharp look and her pale face. I clambered up from the ground in a hurry. Uncertain of what had happened, Sang-Woon and Soon-Bok gazed at me, bursting with curiosity, and whispered,

"Did you see?"

"Did you see?"

I was so scared I couldn't talk, I just quaked.

"Run, we've got to run away."

Whispering thus, I was ready to run, but a moment later it was all over.

The angry face of our teacher, Mr. Kim, was blocking our way.

His hard fist struck me on the face first. Fiery stars shot into my fear-stricken eyes. At that moment I had no chance to consider what might have happened to Sang-Woon or Soon-Bok. Then Mr. Kim grabbed me by the neck, pushed me toward the teachers' room and shouted in an angry voice,

"Inside, all of you!"

We marched into the teachers' room side by side. Once inside, the female teacher was sitting at her desk, but she ignored us, looking out the window. We walked to Mr. Kim's desk, and stood right in front of it.

"Heads up, you sons of bitches!"

It was much harsher and louder than his voice at the morning drills, and the curse was something we had never heard of even at home.

"Ma'am, these rascals are the ones, right?"

His voice changed completely from a harsh shriek to a tender, gentle tone. But his tender voice couldn't ease the woman teacher's rage. She sat for a long time without saying a word. In the hot summer afternoon, the deadly silence sent chills down our spines.

"This place was suffocating as it was, and now I can't stay here any longer."

Her words echoed with deep sorrow. I don't know why, but I finally burst out crying. But the tears I shed weren't tears of regret.

"There's nothing I can do for such kids, helping them is beyond my power."

"But you must understand. They are sons of bastard seamen, so their kinds are wild."

In fear and horror, we had our heads hung low, but we didn't miss a single word passing between the two teachers.

At first we were ordered to kneel until the nerves of our heels went numb. When we were ordered to get up again, none of us could stand up straight. But this punishment wasn't enough to satisfy Mr. Kim's anger. Next, he ordered each of us to fetch a water bucket from the classroom, fill it up with water and bring it back.

The well was located at the end of the playground, next to the principal's garden. The principal, who was working inside a chicken coop, looked up at the loud noise of drawing water from the well.

"Not through with your cleaning, yet? Finish in a hurry, or they'll be worrying about you at home."

At those words from the kind-hearted principal, I felt suffocated with emotion. I turned around with the water bucket before Sang-Woon and Soon-Bok did.

The two teachers were conversing about something in an amiable tone. Judging from the way she had lowered her head, it looked as though Mr. Kim was trying to console her with kind words. When he heard us coming, he glared fearsomely at us, and commanded us to hold the buckets up high above our heads.

It was possible to lift it up for a while, but our strength didn't hold out for very long. The instant a bucket began to move downwards, Mr. Kim would thunder a shout that shook the windowpanes. But the buckets, momentarily lifted again, soon were lowered.

The most painful memory of my otherwise pleasant grammar school years was of holding up the water bucket that day. It was the first time in my life that I paid a penalty for an offense I had committed, though such incidents were commonplace in the military. I may speak of it as a punishment for a crime, but until today I have never felt any remorse about doing it. What was it that I had done? How could I excuse my behavior? How could I explain that the motive which had driven us to peek in the outhouse window was the shock of disbelief?

That was the day that I lost respect for all teachers, a respect that had once verged on adoration of them as mysterious deities. My old pride at being a son of the sea had been deformed into shame at being the son of a bastard seaman. The mystical worship I had so cherished, the pride that only we shared... when these were taken away one by one, we who had been so innocent suddenly became hardened with experience. Our attitudes, reflected in the way we looked at our teachers or our peers, were completely changed from then on. We were preoccupied with the reception of things that were not our own. We began to act like shiftless youths who idle away their time after leaving school, or like petty clerks at some lazy district office. Our changed behavior made us often seem impudent, but the little boys in our class regarded us as most enviable. Not only among the boys, but also among the nice village girls, we knew we were a frequent topic of talk.

A strong awareness that we were sons of bastard seamen in the end served to polarize the class. The principal, who by then was our teacher, didn't sense the change, but we were in a constant struggle with the other kids over some invisible object. It was sad, but now it has become a part of a beautiful memory.

During Marine Corps training and also afterwards as a private, there were many times when I received the old grammar school punishment under the name of "building character". I used to wonder what good so-called character-building would do, as I often wondered what lesson we were being taught by being forced to hold the water bucket over our heads. If Mr.

Kim had only asked us the motive of our conduct before dishing out rigorous punishment to console the lady teacher... if only he could have understood our yearning for the wide open sea of mysterious dreams, could he still have called us names like "sons of bitches" or "sons of bastard seamen"?

In the Marines, every time I was given a severe dose of character building, the same thought recurred to me, as I examined the expression of my superior. It was the only notion left in my mind after long hours of drill were over. A salute is an obligatory gesture towards an identified badge of rank. A badge of rank is not a reliable indication of the person himself, nor of his dignity as a man, but merely a signal. Thus, my eyes were trained to look for the rank before the person or his dignity as a man, and my salute was merely an mechanical acknowledgment of the rank, lacking any true respect.

That day, having mopped up the water we spilled, and before we left the teachers' room and the two young teachers behind us, we each made a solemn pledge to bring our mother or father to school the very next day. It was dark outside, and we were so exhausted we fell down almost with every other step.

The waves had washed away the bobbing light for good. My vision and my hearing, or what I fancied I saw and heard, were totally submerged in darkness. Only then did I return to my senses. I hurried back to the same road I had walked on my way home after that awful ordeal. The visit had another purpose than just to see Kil-Nam's performance in the festival. In a way, I felt I was going to witness my own childhood again.

By the time I arrived at the school, it looked like the first part of the show was already over. As I walked through the gate I saw a cluster of shadows, and quite a crowd was pressing in and out of the building. I had to pause on the playground for a long time, for my lame leg was throbbing, probably due to the fast walk.

It was intermission. Little children who'd been absorbed in the performance were outside, excitedly reenacting what they had seen on the stage. There was still some time before the second act would begin. I thought about saying hello to the principal, and the village elders before the intermission ended, but I was deterred by the formalities involved and decided to stay where I was.

The commotion and noise died down. The little ones were flocking back inside, forming a line like ground spiders. I walked slowly up to the entrance. The hall had already settled down. I stepped in the hall followed by a straggling child. Impure air and pulsing stares greeted me. To avoid those looks, I found a seat close to the door and sank into it. There was still time left before the curtain would lift for the second part.

The murky air and artificial lighting made everything blurry for a while, but as the atmosphere calmed down, I could see more distinctly. Sitting in the front most seat was the principal, behind him was the District Chief, and then the Police Chief. I ran my eyes over the people sitting in the VIP rows. The owner of the mill at the crossroad, who had been elected as a councilman during a by-election, was there. This elderly man with a bald head had a reputation as an extremely agreeable person before he became a councilman, but people said he'd completely changed, like two sides of a hand, ever since the election.

For a long time, I peered at the mill owner who had been transformed into a different man. He looked cross. So, what we once took for an outgoing generosity was just obsequiousness, he had learned to conceal his pride for his own benefit. That he had become the object of gossip among the villagers proved that, after all, he was consciously revealing his long disguised vanity.

A low classroom platform had been elevated to serve as a stage. The very same thing had been done when we had our school play. The mass of faces now shimmering before my eyes seemed the very same crowd of spectators that had gathered in the receding past.

The prop changes weren't yet ready. I imagined I was a little boy, seated backstage, waiting patiently for the curtain to go up. When I realized Kil-Nam had performed in the part I had missed, I was very distressed.

The sound of wooden gong was heard. It was the signal that the curtain would soon rise. The hubbub in the hall was then quieted down. Casually, I looked across to the other side. The Disabled Veterans contingent, in formal dress, waved at me to come and join them. I declined the offer and looked around when my eyes met those of Kil-Nam's mother. I saw a sense of relief in her eyes. She, like her boy, must have been on the lookout for me. For some reason, I felt relieved, too. When our glances crossed, others around us also looked at me. The owner of the general store at the three-corner junction, his fat wife and his daughter, a regular fountain of scandal, were among them.

Looking around the hall, everything seemed to have stayed just as it was, but, simultaneously, any number of things had changed or were in the process of being altered.

First, the principal in the front row proved it. I knew that his baldness was nothing new, but his head looked especially shiny that night.

His face was full of deep wrinkles like a hollow shell, bespeaking his youth there, a life on the shore.

Random applause started to be heard. I looked up at the stage. With the curtain still down, Kil-Nam's teacher was out on stage. I smiled bitterly, seeing the face of our old teacher, Yoo-Cheol Kim, in place of his. Everything has become no more than a memory. In my mind, I can still clearly see Mr. Kim's wife, her baby loaded on her back, as she came to ask the principal where her husband was. He had disappeared with the young woman teacher not long after the Arts Festival. Ugly rumors, embarrassing to repeat, were forever circling in the village and we even had some days off from school because of the unseemly incident.

Kil-Nam's teacher was providing an introduction to the drama about to be performed. The title was "The People of the Stepping Stone Village". The principal, he said, had authored the script, and had even directed it. Waiting for the curtain to rise, I returned to my own school days.

The drama we had done was a history play, also written by the principal himself. "Princess Nang-Nang and Prince Ho-Dong" was the title. We, the cast, were quite immersed in it, but the audience that night was also swept up by a strange excitement. While the scenery was being changed they seemed to savor the sorrow and anguish until the action restarted.

At the lines spoken between the smaller kids, I felt,

again and again, tears welling up in my eyes. The play revealed much more of the hearts of the stepping stone villagers than of the people who lived at the three cornered junction. I saw one woman, recently wed to a son of a village shipowner burst out weeping.

What made me depressed was not just the wretched reality we confronted. Among the faces of the heroes on the stage, I thought I glimpsed the face of one of the three of us. We grew precocious from the time we were punished in the teachers' room with the water bucket method, but what could account for the precociousness of those heroes on the stage now? I was impressed by the way they had memorized the dialogue so perfectly, but what struck me even more was their ability to express the right emotions so accurately.

I closed my eyes for a moment. What was it that had driven the principal to write such a play? Did he want to be a true witness of the stepping stone village? I was gripped by a stifling agony.

The stage backdrop was a blue sea under the gradually sloping hill where the stepping stone stood. It was around twilight, and sound effects of waves enhanced the peacefulness of the dark sea.

Three shadows were stirring. They were sitting in a boat beached on the shore. The one sitting in the middle stood up, and in a low voice said,

"Even if we cast our nets twelve months out of the year and catch all the *jari* we can, it's still a hard life." His body trembled as he looked up at the sky with his arms crossed.

"It's all the same that our lives are at the sea's mercy, but this time, just for this one trip, our luck will change. If we miss this one opportunity, our flesh and bones will rot in the depths of the sea. That was our grandfathers' fate and our fathers', too, remember?" Young-Soo, deep in thought, didn't reply. The wave sound effects were still on.

"Young-Soo, the time for complaints is past, now you must decide what action to take, don't you agree?" The fellow who until then had been silent said to Young-Soo.

"Action?"

Young-Soo retorted, casting a puzzled glare at the other two in turn.

"Right. We want you to decide what you will do."

"Don't you trust me?"

His voice and face both were imbued with sorrow. He paced back and forth for a while, as if to control a pain inside, and went on,

"What can I do when it's already decided? What exactly do you expect me to do?"

"I'm glad to hear it, Young-Soo. That's just what we wanted from you... your resolution".

"As long as you stick to that resolution, we can make it."

Said another fellow as he stood up, in a voice that was soft but full of emotion.

"Well, let's go home now and meet here again later at eleven. A truck will be waiting for us when we unload the goods from the boat. Take this, it was given us as an advance."

Hesitantly, Young-Soo took the roll of money.

The stage darkened while the scene was changed, and during this brief interlude there was a small disturbance in the audience. I looked at Kil-Nam's mother. She had her head down, evidently absorbed in thought. I had to make an effort to control my breathing. The roll of bills taken by Young-Soo up on the stage reminded me, down to the minutest detail, of incident I had taken part in one night years before.

Soon-Bok's death, what took place that night... these were secrets buried deep in my heart. How did the principal, who penned the play, exhume these secrets?

I had never been able to tell Soon-Bok's wife how he died. She might possibly have heard something about the cause of her husband's death from someone else. Preoccupied, her head hanging down, she looked like she was in pain from a deep wound. I couldn't sit there and face it any longer. But what good would remorse do now?

As the new scene was slowly illumined, the stirrings in the audience subsided. I was afraid to watch the performance, but despite my terrible apprehension, I focused all my attention on the stage, like the rest of audience.

Against the background of a thatched hut like those commonly seen in the stepping stone village, the boy playing the role of Young-Soo was standing up, and his wife was sitting a bit behind him. I could almost smell the fishy odors of our village coming from the stage. The scene was on the beach, and a mosquito smoker stood in their yard to scatter the terrible pests. A sense of impatience and uneasiness was displayed in Young-Soo's gestures. His anxious expression and restlessness weighed heavily on the audience. The words of the chief engineer, the "uncle" I encountered during my first shipboard duty, suddenly flashed in mind—he had lost all his money and friends, and the only thing left was the scar on his forehead. If he was left with a scar, what was I left with? Great remorse, unforgettable sorrow... what was I to do with these residues, with the pain and suffering?

The idea of earning money by delivering smuggled goods, and of using the profits to locate Soon-Bok's wife in Incheon or in the red-light district in Seoul.... It was a beautiful friendship, an unfulfilled dream, but today it lingered only as a regret, a reason for weeping. Such a plan never would have occurred to us if Soon-Bok's wife had come back.

On stage, Young-Soo's wife was pleading with her husband not to commit a crime for the sake of money. Young-Soo, initially firm in his resolve, gradually weakened.

"Oaths exchanged among men must be faithfully discharged. If I don't keep my word, it means betrayal."

Young-Soo's voice was imbued with sorrow. After this reply, his wife said no more.

True. Friends should be faithful, and betrayals should never sadden human relations.

Then the voice of Young-Soo's wife rang out sharply,

"Faith is important, but don't you see you're about to betray a greater good for the sake of a lesser?"

Listening to his wife, Young-Soo stared vacantly up at the sky.

"A greater good, a greater good...."

Mumbling the same phrase over and over, he paced back and forth on the stage. The wife, endeavoring to console her husband, pulled him over to sit beside her, and whispered in a calm voice,

"Dear, remember what you said to me before our wedding, when we sat on the hill with the stepping stone? I still cherish in my heart the beautiful dream of that night. There's no suffering I cannot endure, because I've never lost that dream."

Severely pained by his wife's words, Young-Soo put his elbows on his knees and pulled at his hair with both hands. His wife's voice grew even more tender.

"There was a lamp twinkling from a fishing boat on the sea."

Her eyes shone dreaming an ineffable dream.

"You embraced me, kissed me passionately for the first time. Then you pressed your trembling lips to my ear and whispered, "You know the song of Iyŏ Island, don't you?" When I nodded, you called my name and said, "Our ancestors for generations have searched for Iyŏ Island, but it is not to be found out there, this stepping stone where we now sit is Iyŏ Island. Why did our forefathers seek an island overlooked by mapmakers... why couldn't they see that this stepping stone is our own paradise?" From that night on, this stepping stone village has been, just as you said, my paradise, the only utopia of my soul."

Young-Soo was still pulling his hair, speechless.

"While you were in the Marines, if this village hadn't been Iyŏ Island to me, I couldn't have lasted for a single day. If it wasn't our utopia, our souls' paradise, I would never have been able to go on waiting for you. Wasn't it to regain our Iyŏ Island that in the war you fought through the jaws of death and came back to me? How could you mix crime with our stepping stone village, our Iyŏ Island, created and guarded all along by you yourself? Will you trade your once honorable uniform for a convict's blue as the price for your crime... and even if you somehow escape that fate, once our Iyŏ Island is lost we'll never be able to recover it."

Unable to withstand his agony any longer, Young-Soo emitted an uncanny cry as he stood up. I, too, jumped up from my seat. I had no choice but to leave. Oddly enough, the loud gasp on stage seemed to be constricting my own throat.

I walked to the end of the playground where we used to play *gonu* under the willow tree. A merciless wind shook the branches. Over the fence was the main road. When we tired of playing, we used to climb over the fence to walk home along that road.

The principal's residence, with no light on, was dimly visible like an indistinct India-ink drawing. In the darkness, I heard a dog barking fiercely in my direction. I was uneasy and my heart burdened. Where had the bald principal dug up the scenario for the play? Our restless quest certainly underlay it. From where had our secret leaked out?

The play was still proceeding, for the brightly lit school building showed no sign of any bustle. But, what was happening? A new illusion floated before my eyes as I stood there in the dark. The young couple standing side by side on the hill with the stepping stone were no longer the Young-Soo and wife I had just seen, they were transformed into Soon-Bok and his wife. Their dialogue floated into my ears like an echo, and it, too, was different than the lines exchanged between Young-Soo and his wife.

I knew that Soon-Bok and she had been seeing each other secretly for about a year before they got married.

Soon-Bok had probably told her in a whisper the legend of Iyŏ Island, with her batting her bright, magical eyes as she listened. They probably swore never to search the sea for Iyŏ Island, and instead to make the stepping stone village their own paradise, a sanctuary of their love. I couldn't help feeling hazy as though my blood was all surging up into my head. That night, I understood at last why Soon-Bok refused to set foot on land until the day he died.

Everyone who saw Soon-Bok leading such an outlandish life, from the day of his return from the service, said he had gone out of his mind. They always advanced two reasons: he had suffered severe shock in battle and his wife had run away. But I think the pivotal reason was that he had lost Iyŏ Island, the most precious thing of all for him.

He sang the song of Iyŏ Island as he rowed, and those indescribable eyes of his as he sang... he desperately tried to rediscover Iyŏ Island, the island for which our ancestors always yearned and searched, every time they put out to sea.

Black clouds darkened the night. No winds breathed on the sea. We rowed. Soon-Bok's boat song, was it the only premonition of his death? Never had I heard such a mournful dirge.

When I first raised the subject of carrying contraband for smugglers, Soon-Bok said nothing. But I kept pressing him. He remained indifferent. So I suggested we could search for his wife in Incheon or in Seoul with our cut of the deal. Only then did he grin a bit. What could that smile mean? I never deciphered it. It sounds feeble; I was in no great need of money myself, it just seemed if we seized the chance, I was sure we'd make a big pile of cash at one go. Then we could follow any and every path on earth to track down his wife, it would be an adventure like when we went to sea.

The promise of this new adventure was stolen away by the waves, and now a black sorrow darker than the clouds over the sea that night, is the violent force assailing my heart.

When we reached the middle of the sea, Soon-Bok's boat song stopped. The oars still in his hands he was glaring at the darkness. I'll never forget how his eyes shone as he stared into the night. What did he see in that darkness? The moment he dropped the oars, the boat shook slightly, but even then the thought never entered my head. He leapt into the water. Was it to find a mysterious new dream, or to recover the beautiful dream he had lost? His suicide was an enigma to everyone.

I spent the restless night on the sea, without a wink of sleep. The next morning I went back to the village with Soon-Bok's body aboard. Everyone readily accepted my account, they even commended me for going to the trouble of retrieving the corpse. But their consolations didn't help me to forget my many wrongs. Who would have guessed that to this day I would be suffering such pain and anguish? Who would share this pain and anguish with me?

The cold wind still whipped the branches, but I stood there motionless, as if I'd turned to stone.

If only Soon-Bok's wife had been back, if she had implored me half as much Young-Soo's wife did to stop her husband, most of all, if only Soon-Bok had said a word …. No amount of regrets could resurrect the lost happiness.

Soon-Bok's body had floated to the surface the next morning. That moment was forever engraved on my memory. I expected he had drifted far away, and never thought his body would reappear there. Drowned bodies are usually bloated and grotesque, but in Soon-Bok's case, he looked like a man asleep, except saturated with water. Not only was he not disfigured, there was even a knowing smile at the corners of his mouth. That night, I racked my brain to interpret the cryptic grin on his dead face, to divine the cause that had driven him to take his own life.

Regardless what anybody thought, Soon-Bok's death was certainly a happy one. Unless his heart had been content, it was unlikely his eyes would have remained closed as in sleep. What, then, had been in Soon-Bok's mind at the moment he jumped into water, and what had his eyes seen in the darkness which drove him into the depths? Could it have been his wife? Did the spectre before his eyes lure him into the water to spare him from falling into an unjust accusation? Or had he seen a vision of the Iyŏ Island he had so long been seeking?

I had to abandon all the ideas I had assembled, for the mere posing of a question to be answered struck me as a self-deceptive rationalization. I was horrified by my own conceit. Soon-Bok's death, after all, didn't seem to be as romantic as my speculations assumed. Once again, I thought of the couple whispering to one another before the stepping stone. The oaths had turned out to be only futile words, and Soon-Bok was left alone, longing for his lost love. Even though it all seemed a vain dream, it was not the fault of Soon-Bok. There must have been something else he kept in his heart that he constantly sought from without. Could the object of his search have been his own resolution to prevent his oath from being revealed as only vain words? Against his will, he probably had to relinquish that oath.

I was the one who came up with the idea of picking up goods from smugglers. I am sure he lacked the courage to decline my proposal. Why didn't he, even once, share his agony with me before leaping all by himself? Who could have sensed the agony he endured when, after rowing the boat that far, he could neither surrender the old oath nor accept a friend's proposal?

The play must have been over. There was a noisy crowd of people coming down toward the playground. Shadows split from the crowd and disappeared through the gate in twos and threes. Among them was one fellow who was loudly reciting the dialogue he'd heard on the stage. I saw two shadows approaching me. From the way they walked, I knew it was the principal and his wife. I had to go, for I didn't have the presence of mind to greet them properly if we crossed paths.

I walked slowly to the gate. The classroom lights went out one by one. Only the shadows of older students could be seen cleaning up the aftermath. Most who had passed through the gate had split into two groups on the road. Those headed downward were from the stepping stone village. The junction community was within easy walking distance of the school, but it was a good two miles down to my village.

With a long walk ahead, people were hurrying their steps. I could hear them talking, but couldn't make them out in the dark.

How did the play end? Naturally, Young-Soo was

persuaded by his wife, but what pain did he suffer for betraying his promise to his friends, and how did his wife ease his pain? Such were my thoughts as I walked along the road. Then, suddenly, I heard her voice coming from the darkness.

"You're late, I thought you left early."

"Yes, ah, well, ..."

Even I knew it was a feeble reply. She and I walked on side by side. She was probably ahead of me, and realizing I was behind her, must have paused to wait for me. Her kindness only aggravated the pain I was feeling at that moment.

No matter how slowly I walked, she constantly dropped behind. Only then did I realize she was carrying Kil-Nam on her back.

"Is he asleep?"

"Yes. When the play was almost over, he grumbled that you had gone, and then fell asleep."

I took Kil-Nam from her and carried him on my own back. The cold wind struck my cheeks, but my heart was warm. We walked and walked, almost forgetting ourselves.

At the sound of waves rolling in and out, we realized our village was near. A sense of something being unfinished lingered in my heart. I wished we had farther to walk. This wish may have stemmed from a need to lessen my aching heart by telling her the details I'd never divulged about Soon-Bok's death.

"Thanks, he's very heavy...."

As we arrived at her front yard, she spoke quietly and took Kil-Nam off my back. For some reason I didn't want to part with him. That body warmth that welded him to my back... I was ecstatic, experiencing in that warmth an indescribable emotion.

Fog and darkness pervaded the village. After she took Kil-Nam from me, I kept standing there for a long time. Not only did it remind me of a scene we had acted in the Arts Festival drama, it sent me back to that precise moment in the past.

The Classroom

With the advent of winter, everything in the village totally changed. The wind that swept over the hill changed, as did the moonlight that escorted the rising tide. That wasn't all. The sky might be high and clear, but the village, even then, became dark and dismal. That particular year was far from usual.

In the dreary shade, you couldn't help but be depressed, and the short days and long nights made it even worse. The gloomy depression led to dire moods, barren and wretched states of mind. Even the sea, usually priding itself in its mystery and romance, was not immune from the general malaise. The once stately waves now whipped about like the tail of an ill-tempered beast, calling to mind a ferocious woman's dagger glances out of the corners of her eyes. That may explain why the villagers seldom ventured out to sea in the winter. On the rare occasions when they went out, they would come back with empty boats. Winter's "poor catches" forced us to survive on wild rye or beans from the hillside, reducing us to the most abject poverty.

The villagers, having grown up in such conditions, had no complaints. Resignation had become second nature with them. By the time winter arrived food was scarce, and it was not unusual for them to borrow from the shipowners, hoping the following spring or summer would bring enough money to repay the loans. Though the village scene was thus dismal, the people were still lively, constantly bustling about.

The winter sky was usually clear and blue, but sometimes the icy wind would bring a heavy fog, dropping a thick curtain over the village. In the mornings, the village looked dreary when freezing mist hung over it. On those days, sleet often fell around dawn, bringing a sense of unrest to the otherwise peaceful village. Dogs, awake before their masters, would race in groups all over the village, barking loud enough to wake the dead. Those were mornings when I woke with foreboding. The sound of dogs' howling somehow made me fretful. I would go outside to calm myself, but the cloudy, gray weather brought only melancholy.

Standing in our front yard, I summoned my dog with a shout. Usually he jumped all over me, wagging his tail, at the mere sound of my footsteps, but when he was out, running wild with his playmates, he ignored my calls. Still I shouted his name at the top of my voice until my black mood lifted. But then, seeing no trace of him, I would again grow sad, for no reason. With no excuse to cry, I would just flop down in the middle of the front yard. Then I would look about, tears by then collecting in my chilled eyes. I would hastily wipe them away with the tip of my finger lest someone notice. Then, oblivious of my surroundings, I would scrawl strange figures along the cracks in the frozen ground. What I felt wasn't exactly like missing some-

one, like the sense of loss I used to feel when I lost at
gonu, the game we played in the summer in the shade
of willow trees on the playground. I found myself un-
consciously drawing an ocean chart in an attempt to
plot the mysterious place where we had drifted at sea.
The mysterious dream we alone had seen and felt...
I absorbed myself in an imaginary quest, thinking that
if only we once more could hold the halyard, we would
surely be able to find the place once more. The broken
cracks on the frozen ground seldom reached beyond
the fence. This led me to a new recognition... the
region we had been seeking was, like the cracks running only up to the fence, somewhere within the horizon and its overarching cumulus clouds.

Time and again I felt immense regret. After all, we
had returned after repeated failures because we lacked
patience. I could no longer stay sitting on the ground.
Stretching my back, I would rise and look out at the
sea. The sleet usually stopped before it even coated the
tiny yard. On a cloudy day like that there was no way I
could see the sea. Only the sound of the waves broke
the morning stillness. On those days, if the sea beyond
the shoreline had been visible, I would probably have
run down, cast anchor and sailed away, without a second thought. It was always the gray weather that
restrained my spirit of adventure and undercut my
self-confidence.

By the time I succumbed to lethargy, oblivious even
to my obsession with the sea adventure, John would
dash in from nowhere and jump all over me. Suddenly
reminded of the sources of my agitation and restlessness, I would kick John away. But he was not deterred
by my apparent hatred. He would turn away after be-

ing kicked so badly that his nose was bloodied but then he would somehow change his mind and come back. In the end, he got angry, too, and would bite my trouser leg and not let it go. Then I'd grab him by the neck, and wrestle with him to see who was the stronger. At first, we hugged each other affectionately, but in the end we would always part in hatred. Worn down by his persistence, I would end up hugging his head and crying. My tears, now that I think of it, were not tears of sorrow from defeat. Those times, my mother usually ran out from the kitchen to help me. John, thrashed with an iron poker, would flee, yelping out mournful cries even more pitiful than mine, and then I would head down the frozen road to school, bookbag on my back and my mother scolding me from behind.

By the time I came back home from school, I usually had figured out what the premonition of the morning meant. We always left school late, and not because we were dismissed late. The distance from school to home was great. School was normally over by midday, but we rarely came straight home. From early spring through late fall, no matter how early we finished school, the walk home was quite tolerable, but winter was an entirely different story. The school furnished only enough fuel for the stove in our classroom to keep us warm for the first hour in the morning, so we used to gather up dry branches and sticks on our way to school, hide them under the platform or behind our desks, and burn them until midday. But there was never enough fuel to keep the stove stoked after school was out. Besides, the school authorities firmly prohibited such use of the stove as being a fire hazard. Consequently, as soon as the class ended we had to

leave the school. Once through the gate, the younger
kids, especially the first graders, might put on their
mothers' thick socks in place of gloves. Often they rushed home crying, unable to bear the freezing weather.
Despite the awful cold, Soon-Bok, Sang-Woon and I
hated to go home early. In those days we used to look
for bits of torn nets. They were not too hard to find.
Then we sewed the torn bits together, and on our way
to school would set traps in bushes where meadow
buntings seemed likely to turn up.

At school, we were often distracted with thoughts of
the meadow buntings that we might have already
caught in the traps. After school, we would creep our
way to the bushes. Seldom did we find as many
meadow buntings as we had imagined during class.
Sometimes only a few were in the traps, five or six at
most. We were like the village fishermen who went to
sea only to return with empty holds.

That was just about all we used to do from after
school let out until sunset. First, we cleaned the
meadow buntings, plucking off all their feathers, slit-
ting their bellies with our fathers' fishing knives, taking
the guts out. Then, we'd make a fire on the hillside, or
on some rock, and roast the birds. In early spring, it
was quite nice to nibble on roasted eggs, but the taste
of roast meadow bunting in the freezing winter was
heavenly indeed. It was always dark by the time we
finished our delectable meal, licked our frozen lips,
and set the traps for the next day.

The routine in winter was always the same. When I
returned home late, ominous happenings always unfolded in the dim light. On cloudy days, especially
when dawn saw sleet, it was the custom to have a

drinking bout. Everyone was poor, borrowing their daily bread from the shipowners, so nobody could afford to treat others as was the custom during "good catch" season. Instead, people gathered around, gambling to decide who'd have to buy the spirits. Whoever lost, by whatever means, had to buy the drinks. There was no way out of it. No matter how badly off he might be, he couldn't ever allow himself to lose face. Since the drinks came not from any genuine hospitality but from the need to save face, an invisible animosity enveloped the drinking table instead of a jovial mood. Therefore, unlike in summer, in winter the drinks would often let to be a besotted frenzy or to a fight.

It was after dark when I came home on that day. The house was usually lit by the time I arrived, but that day it was still dark. When I walked in the door, my mother called me from the kitchen. I asked her why no light was on, but she asked me to be quiet, beckoning me to come into the kitchen. Just then I heard a strange moaning sound coming from the other room. Father was groaning in his sleep. It was a faint sound, yet I could tell he was greatly agitated. I could also smell a strong odor of wine. It wasn't difficult to picture my father sprawled in the dark room, completely drunk. I knew then why my mother had called me in a quiet voice. If he was awakened in his drunken state, the whole family would fall victim to his drunkenness. I went into the kitchen.

My mother was making a fire to heat the room. Her face, lit by the flames, made me feel sad. Unable to look at her swollen eyes, I squatted down in front of the hearth, and asked,

"Something happened?"

"Hurry and grow up."

She murmured as if to herself, giving me the rice and soup that had been waiting on the earthen stove. It was as I had expected. There had been a drinking bet early that day, and father, having lost the bet, had to pay for all the drinks to keep from losing face. But, knowing how badly we were doing at home, he couldn't have felt very good about it. It so happened that my father had gotten into a fight with Sang-Woon's father that day. Drinks and fights were a part of life in our village, but it surprised me to hear there had been a fight between them, of all people. Just as the three of us were bosom buddies, my father and Sang-Woon's father were known around the village as the closest of friends. It was incomprehensible. How could they have a fight? There was liquor to blame, still I couldn't believe it.

After a bowlful of rice mixed with soup, I was weary and drooping from exhaustion. In front of the warm fire I felt like dozing off. My mother repeated what she had said earlier,

"I hope you hurry and grow up."

Her words sounded far away to me, like some fairy tale of long ago. Today I often think of those words heard when I was half asleep. What could've been my mother's lost hope, my mother who resented reality, and whose resentment in the end became resignation?

"I hope you hurry and grow up."

Her resentment and resignation led her to hold great expectations for my future.

Now I am thinking of my mother's death. She passed away before I grew up to be a man. Where, then, did her true happiness lie? Just as my joyous wish was bound up with a search for a mysterious sea, her dream may have centered on the days long ago when she fed me from her breasts. After such a train of thought, I wondered about Kil-Nam and his mother, Soon-Bok's wife. I had never heard her say so, but it seemed most likely she found her life's meaning only in Kil-Nam's future. Burdened with such thoughts, my heart felt suffocated. To free myself from this oppression, I went to sea at all hours.

Growing up in such conditions, not only did we come home from school late, the minute we woke up in the morning we rushed off to school. The sun barely had begun to shed its rays by the time we reached the bushes. It was the best time for catching meadow buntings. We would pluck them on the spot, stuff them in our pockets and go on to school. By the time we arrived at school, our frozen fingertips would feel better from the warmth of the birds.

Even in summer, the children from the junction area rarely brought their lunches because they lived close enough to go home for lunch. But children from the stepping stone village brought their lunch from late spring till late autumn, though when the weather turned cold it wasn't possible. That a cold lunch in winter would make you sick at your stomach was the reason, but it was merely a pretext to save face in the presence of the kids from town. At home, our food had run out and we had to borrow from the shipowner to eat at all. We simply couldn't afford lunch. The meadow buntings we trapped on the way to school were in place of lunch. The kids from the junction were rather meek, not nearly as tough as us. We weren't allowed to roast our birds on the stove when we got to school in the morning. Earlier that winter, we did roast them before the first class, but because of the nasty stench in the classroom, we were scolded by our teacher. But during the lunch hour, the teacher might frown at the smell, but didn't say much, thinking it was just the aroma of our lunches being warmed.

Our birds were the most popular food in our class, and we could trade them for the town children's corn on the cob or roasted beans. Some of them, usually boys, even begged us to swap our birds for their rice-cakes.

We were more mature and bolder than the children from the junction, and somehow that didn't make us very popular among the girls in class. They giggled at us, regarding us as barbarians, but we feigned indifference. In fact, it was usual to accost the girls when they acted silly like that. But we ignored their frivolousness because we weren't from the town. Nothing happened when a fight broke out among the town kids, but if we ever so much as snarled at one of those girls, it caused a great row. They would burst into tears, and run straight to the teachers' room, which meant we would soon be summoned there. So, it was, all things considered, wisest to ignore those girls. It was after being punished for peeking through the outhouse window that we really grew magnanimous. Our classmates generally were friendly to us, but we didn't share any close ties with them. Their eagerness to get to know us had become much more pronounced since our foray out to sea. True, the town children didn't know much about the sea, but it was only after we had undertaken that totally unexpected adventure that they felt irresistably attracted to us. Whenever we sat together around the fire, they asked us endless questions about the sea, and especially about that day. We were never able to answer their questions to their satisfaction, somehow.

As I said earlier, our school was co-ed, and the fifth and sixth grades were put together in one class. There were only four girls in the sixth year. They were Kil Gop-Soon, whose family owned a tobacco shop at the junction, Chang Kil-Ja, Kim Myung-Sook and Lee Hyo-Sook. There were about ten girls in the fifth grade, but as they didn't interest me, I don't recall any of their names. Of the four older girls, the tobacco shop owner's daughter, Kil Gop-Soon, was the one who was most preoccupied with us. She was always forward and aggressive. Chang Kil-Ja, on the other hand, who also was very enthralled with us, had the gift of hiding her curiosity.

There was always a keen sense of competition mixed with restraint, probably because it was a mixed class of the fifth and sixth graders containing both boys and girls. Considering the distance, we should have arrived at school after the children from town, but we were always the first there. Even our early arrival at school was among us a matter of competition. It was understood that whoever arrived first would enjoy the exclusive right to warm themselves next to the stove.

Winning a place by the stove was extremely competitive between the girls and us. Whichever side occupied the place first, then the other had to give in. The few times we gave up our spoils, it was because of the tobacco shop owner's daughter.

One day, frozen by the icy wind, we walked in the classroom triumphantly as the first comers, only to find Kil Gop-Soon and Chang Kil-Ja warming themselves before the fire. At that instant, our confident expectations evaporated. We, who had walked in so proudly, could do nothing but look at each other in silence. I noticed a strange grin on Gop-Soon's face when she noticed our halting embarrassment. It was a complacent smile, challenging us to take over the fire if we could. That happened more than once. It was exceedingly unpleasant. If only she had said something to us, it would've been different. Sang-Woon and Soon-Bok must have felt the same way. We put our bookbags inside our desks and were about to turn around when Chang Kil-Ja got up and walked over to her desk.

"Kil-Ja, stay here."

Gop-Soon's tone was imperious, but Kil-Ja ignored it. Then I realized what Chang Kil-Ja's action meant. Undoubtedly, she meant to offer her place to us, just in from the cold. I saw Soon-Bok and Chang Kil-Ja look at each other, and Soon-Bok, for no apparent reason, blushed. Without taking a moment to look closely at their faces I turned away myself, for I was, in a strange way, shocked. That Soon-Bok, who could stare with equanimity at Gop-Soon, turned red at a mere glance from Chang Kil-Ja, meant there was something between them, and I was glad to know there was. On the other hand, I felt a sort of jealousy that Soon-Bok had kept it a secret even from us.

"Shit...."

I don't remember who said it. It must have been Soon-Bok or Sang-Woon. Anyhow, we ran outside, leaving that vulgar pronouncement behind.

On the playground, it was especially windy that

day. Once outside, I chanced to look back at the class-room. Chang Kil-Ja, who I thought had gone back to her seat, was standing at the window, looking at us. I craned my neck, which had been retracted like a turtle's, and shouted,

"Hey, let's play horse riding."

There we were with no particular plan in mind, so they excitedly took up my suggestion. I was grateful for their enthusiasm. If we had been seen shivering in the cold out on the playground, she would have felt sorry for us, and my pride couldn't bear such pity.

In high spirits, we began the game. Scissors, rock, paper, scissors, rock, paper, and in the end Sang-Woon was the horse and I, the horseman, led the horse while Soon-Bok sat atop it. There was a peculiar tension among us. I, more than the others, grew especially tense when I felt Chang Kil-Ja's gaze falling on us through the window. The nervousness I felt then to this day is something I cannot explain.

The cold wind was biting at the tips of our noses, but the eyes of the rider Soon-Bok, mysteriously shone. It wasn't merely pride of being the rider. I kept wondering about it as I led the horse. Soon-Bok didn't fail to sense my distraction and seized just the right moment suddenly to mount the horse. Once in the saddle, the rider would display his daring by raising both arms high up in the air. It wasn't the horse but the horseman who was to blame if the knight didn't fall while mounting the horse. Each time Soon-Bok was given the chance to jump up on the horse without mishap. Soon-Bok once more successfully mounted the steed and let out a yell.

"So, you made it again, what's there to shout

about?"

"Come on, see if you can make me fall."

Soon-Bok was wagging his bottom in triumph, but I wasn't in a good mood at all. It wasn't so much because I was stuck playing the horseman the whole time. I was smitten by envy as I saw Soon-Bok showing off to his heart's content for the benefit of Chang Kil-Ja, who was watching us through the window.

Meanwhile we forgot entirely about the cold. The principal, our teacher, who was on his way to school just then, passed us by. We stopped our game to give him a polite bow.

"You should be inside warming yourselves in this weather...." But we had no interest in responding to that, and went on with our game. The younger kids, their necks and ears all wrapped with scarves, didn't go straight into the classroom, and instead surrounded us to watch our game.

The bell rang. The little ones at once swarmed into the classroom. We weren't cold at all. In fact, our bodies were soaked with sweat. When we walked in the classroom, the hot air of the room felt stuffy. Before the teacher arrived, we wiped off the sweat with our bookbags but, embarrassingly enough, the perspiration kept on streaming down our faces.

Sang-Woon and Soon-Bok both sat on the next row ahead, diagonally from my seat. A light steam was emanating from their backs. Thinking I must be in the same shape, I rubbed my head and the sweat rained down in my open book like cold drops of dew. But, soon the stuffy warmth was replaced by a sudden chill running up our spines. By then the teacher had started calling on pupils to read aloud sections he had read through once. To be honest, though my book was open in my hands, my head felt fuzzy and I was half asleep. At the sound of my name being called, I was suddenly jerked back to my senses, but it was already too late. The whole class quaked with laughter. A friend sitting beside me gave me a nudge, pointing out the part I was supposed to read, and I had to get up then and there and rattle it off. Then one more roar of laughter would erupt, for in my muddled state I started to read the wrong line.

To us the teacher always looked stern, but at those moments he was so ferocious looking that my head would drop. My face burnt hotter than when I sweated in the sun, and I had to struggle not to shed tears like when blasted by a frigid gale.

"What do you mean by dozing off in the first period? Still not quite awake, I suppose. Take your book out in the hall, and stay there until you're wide awake!"
No sooner had he finished speaking than I grabbed my book and rushed out. I was lucky. I preferred not to be summoned to the front of the class, and scolded there before everybody. Besides, I was glad he caught me, and not Soon-Bok. While it is true I'd felt an inexplicable envy during the horse-riding game, being punished was another matter entirely.

The hall was as cold as outside. Both ends were open, so wind blew through unchecked. My hands and feet both went numb as I stood there freezing, and then at last the bell rang. On such occasions, the same old hour of class seemed unbelievably long. After the bell, the teacher wound up the class and went straight over to his office. And as soon as the teacher walked out, Soon-Bok would rush out before anybody else to hug me and pull me back into the classroom.

"Nasty cold, wasn't it?"

The tenderness in his gentle voice thawed my frozen body at once. When I shook my head as if it had been nothing, Sang-Woon would urge,

"Warm yourself at the fire."

Then Soon-Bok would take exception to Sang-Woon's suggestion,

"No, he shouldn't. It's bad to warm frostbitten hands at a fire, can be very painful."

I sat in bliss between two dear friends, one urging me to go near the fire and the other advising me to stay celar of it, and Chang Kil-Ja watched our touching mutual concern with envy.

It was the coldest day of that winter. When we entered the main gate, even our eyelashes were frozen. We knew that on a cold day like that there would be lots of meadow buntings in our traps, but the bitter cold drove us straight to school. Needless to say, we were the ones who staked claims on the stove on that morning. The school seemed deserted, and the maintenance man must have just lit the fire. We threw our bookbags on the desks and huddled around the stove, trying to make a good fire. The classroom filled up with smoke. Only then the coal in the stove began to glow red. We cleared away some debris and sat around the stove. The frost flowers blooming on the window-panes began slowly melting away at the sharp rise in the room temperature. You couldn't see outside very well through those windows. The three of us did a good job of wiping the dripping panes clean. Even the wind that made the branches shake as it blew past was now visible, but not another soul had walked through the gate yet. The classroom was quiet except for the sound of our breathing and the sound of the fire crackling. Suddenly, we all turned to face the door as it opened with a ponderous creak. I don't know why I was so perplexed to see Chang Kil-Ja walk in. What could have happened? Up to then I had been keeping an eye on the main gate, and hadn't seen her come in. I was embarrassed. If only I'd known she'd be coming that early I would have saved a place for her. I looked at Soon-Bok. From his blushing, I knew he was thinking the same thing. For some reason, the normally prim Chang Kil-Ja smiled as she crossed the room to her desk. Sang-Woon and Soon-Bok were the first to turn back to face the stove. As if nothing had happened, I too turned my back to her, but her presence set all my nerves on edge.

"It's cold, come here by the fire."

Those were the words on the tip of my tongue, but somehow I couldn't speak. For a while, silence reigned. After arranging her books in order, Chang Kil-Ja came over by us. I shifted my chair to one side, making room for her. But, she paid no heed to my gesture and walked over to Sang-Woon and Soon-Bok and whispered to them, rubbing her hands together near the stove flue.

"Cold, isn't it? Seems like the coldest day all winter. I knew you would already be here."

None of us could muster a word in reply.

"Right, It's the coldest. So, we came directly to school without even stopping by the bushes to collect our meadow buntings."

Sang-Woon said. I a was little annoyed that Sang-Woon told her why we didn't stop at the traps, and I

didn't understand what she meant by saying she knew
we'd be there already.

"Well, then I'm saved! Today I won't have to endure
that nasty smell."

She blushed as she teased us.

"You really hate the smell that much?"

"Yes. I don't know about the others, but I certainly
dislike it."

If anyone other than she had said it, I probably
could've come up with some retort, but I was at a loss
to contradict her.

"Try this today instead of the meadow buntings, you
can roast it, too."

She took out a good-sized paper bag and handed it to
Soon-Bok.

"What's this?"

As he took the bag Soon-Bok's eyes shone even brighter
than yesterday when he was the rider.

"Beans."

She spoke softly like a shy bride. Sang-Woon grinned, looking out the corners of his eyes at the bag in
Soon-Bok's hands. But I was chagrined.

"Don't I get any?"

My discontent finally emerged into the open.

"You all can share it, can't you?"

Her already blushed face reddened even more as she
lowered her eyes. But it didn't look like Soon-Bok was
about to share the contents of the bag. By then students
began appearing at the main gate. Having given the
bag to Soon-Bok, Chang Kil-Ja returned to her desk
like nothing had happened. Only then did I realized
why she had come to school so unusually early. Everyone entering through the gate was in a great hurry, all

bundled up to the ears with scarves. The place was getting chaotic. I peered out the window and pictured the little ones trudging all the way from the stepping stone village. Over the hill, and crossing the frozen rye field, a short cut, they probably had tripped and fallen into the uneven furrows time and again. When sunlight began to shower in, a feeling of uneasiness always descended, as if school had already begun. The little ones often burst into tears when strong gusts of wind blew them off balance or unwrapped their scarves. But they still made it to school, even if crying all the way. I couldn't help smiling as I watched the smallest kids coming through the gate, showing not a trace of the rough trip they had just finished.

As the sound of the classroom door opening and closing became noisier, the temperature in the room gradually fell. The frozen breath on their eyelids melted, making their faces look like beautiful, dew-soaked morning flowers. Each time they exhaled, a whitish steam rose up into the air. Now that we were completely warmed up, we were expected to surrender our spots by the fire to them.

The bell rang before the late comers had had time to warm themselves. We went to our respective seats before the teacher walked in.

Footsteps were heard out in the hall, stopping before our classroom. The class all at once became as a calm sea. The door opened and the teacher walked in. But then a commotion broke out in the room. Here and there whispers could be heard. Surely, our teacher had come to school that morning, so what was going on? The commotion was because the teacher who had just walked in was not our own, but the woman who taught the first and second grades. She stepped up on the platform, and the class finally quieted down.

"The principal is busy with preparations for the Arts Festival, so I'll be in charge of this period today."

At the words "Arts Festival", the class once more stirred. To bring order to the class, the teacher began to read our Korean Reader. But the unfamiliar voice made us even more restless. About the time this unruly class was over, the principal showed up. At the same time, the woman teacher left the room. ·

On the platform, the teacher looked us over as usual, and stiffening his neck, said in a solemn voice,

"This year, as always, our school will have an Arts Festival. I was detained by preparations for the event." Here he paused, and looked at some papers he had brought with him before continuing. We knew right away that it was the script for the play to be performed at the Festival.

"The play we will perform this year is an historical drama based on the lives of Prince Ho-Dong and Princess Nang-Nang."

He began in this way his introduction of the play, and unlike his dry delivery in history class, he talked as though he was telling a folk tale. When he finished with an outline of the play, the whole class was in a tumult. Some were stamping the floor, some screaming their lungs out, and some even drumming on their books with both hands. The class deteriorated into a pandemonium, but the teacher kept smiling as if quite content. When the bedlam subsided a bit, he went on,

"Now, the question is, which of you will play the leading roles?"

At these words from him, the class suddenly fell silent.

We all looked about like we each had someone in mind for the parts. When the teacher spoke again, he had everyone's undivided attention.

"So, after some discussion with the other teachers, I've chosen the following persons...."

The teacher called out the names of the cast one by one. Mostly sixth grade students and a few from the fifth grade. But our curiosity was not yet satisfied. We wanted to know who would get to play the leading roles. At that moment, Gop-Soon, the tobacconist's daughter, stood up.

"Sir, I would like to play the role of Princess Nang-Nang."

Her face was nearly crimson from excitement. The teacher grinned and nodded, but said nothing. It seemed somehow to be an unspoken commitment to give her the role of the princess. Then I heard another voice, no less daring than that of Gop-Soon. I could tell it was Soon-Bok's voice. His jeering was open and unabashed. Similar responses broke out here and there. Gop-Soon's face turned beet red as she sat back down.

"Well, let me now fix the leading roles. To make it fair, I have chosen two actors for each role. The one who memorizes the lines better and speaks in a clear voice will get the part."

I looked at Gop-Soon and Chang Kil-Ja in turn. In my opinion, they were the only two who could possibly play the princess. Gop-Soon looked the teacher straight in the face, beaming with confidence, but Chang Kil-Ja had been hanging her head from the beginning. As I expected, Gop-Soon and Chang Kil-Ja were named for the role of Princess Nang-Nang, and for Prince Ho-Dong he selected Soon-Bok and Young-Soo, son of the owner of the cotton gin at the junction.

After the leading roles were announced, I was disappointed, but still I was glad for Soon-Bok. The players took copies of the script home to study for the rehearsal on the following day. It so happened that it was our turn that day to do the sweeping after school, and we could stay as late as we wanted. We roasted the beans Chang Kil-Ja had given us in the morning, and, neglectful of our cleaning duties, began learning the dialogues by heart. Fortunately, or unfortunately, there wasn't a single line for the Prince's servant, which was the role assigned to me. While Soon-Bok and Sang-Woon were absorbed in memorizing their lines, I went up on the platform and spent some time improvising the carriage and gait fitting for a Prince's servant.

Remembrance

On the way home we didn't stop by the bushes for the meadow buntings, and the next day we again went straight to school. None of us ever brought up the subject of the birds again. In fact, our days of hunting meadow buntings came to an end, as a practical matter, as soon as Chang Kil-Ja had spoken about the smell.

School let out after second period on the following day, and, except for students with parts in the play, everyone was sent home because there were to be tryouts within the cast for the leading roles. We all sat around the stove, and the principal presided over the audition. Of the three teachers, the one in charge of the third and fourth grades didn't come, but the woman teacher was there. We looked at the competitors who would be fighting over the roles of the Prince and Princess. They looked at least as excited as us. I was more concerned about Chang Kil-Ja than about my best friend, Soon-Bok. I was nervous due to fear that the role of the Princess would very likely fall to Gop-Soon instead of Chang Kil-Ja. The preparation for the audition was complete when seats for the two teachers were placed in front of the platform. Then, one at a time, we were called out onto the stage. Gop-Soon was the first to go.

With all eyes greedily watching her, Gop-Soon looked at the ceiling and began to recite her lines. It was the scene where the Princess was in agony after reading a message from Prince Ho-Dong, delivered by a courier of Koguryo Kingdom.

Beloved Princess,
How I have longed to be with you! Yet, I am tormented by the drum which your father, the King, treasures most. How can I dare go to a place where every single move I make will be closely watched by the drum? My dearest, my heart, I implore you to burn the drum, your father's most precious treasure, then I shall greet you as my wife. If not, I must remain here, forever without you.

Having finished the message, Gop-Soon, for a brief moment, turned her eyes from the ceiling to us. After a deep breath, she went on:
"What am I to do! My father treasures the drum more than his own daughter.... Am I to abandon my father and myself, or shall I abandon my beloved?"
Drowning in an unfathomable sorrow, the Princess

spoke this soliloquy as she stealthily crept to the pavilion where the drum was kept. We half lost ourselves listening to her. The principal wore a thin smile the whole time she was speaking. After her reading Gop-Soon bowed politely to the two teachers and came back over by us. What did the principal's thin smile mean? I felt uneasy, because I had the impression that his smile meant he had already decided to assign the role of the Princess to Gop-Soon. It was apparent that the clever girl, based on the principal's smile and the general mood, was certain of her success. Chang Kil-Ja's turn was next. I prayed for her success. When Chang Kil-Ja stepped up on the platform, both the principal and the lady teacher looked at her with nervous expression.

At last she began to recite the same lines. She didn't merely stare at the ceiling like Gop-Soon had, I noticed her changing her glances from situation to situation, and her facial expressions varied as well. The dreadful sorrow of the Princess...it wasn't just heard in the lines, it was visible through the expressiveness of her whole body. When the recitation was over, it sounded like the spectators were exhaling after holding their breath. The children seated around the stove looked at Chang Kil-Ja, who had just finished her lines, then at Gop-Soon, and back at Chang Kil-Ja again. Nobody had thought that the quiet, introvert Chang Kil-Ja had such a gift hidden inside. Our teacher also seemed greatly surprised. The two teachers quickly exchanged some words, and though I couldn't hear them, I readily guessed they were praising Chang Kil-Ja's talent. But they didn't yet announce the winner of the audition for the role of the Princess, and went on with the role of the Prince.

Soon-Bok was first up on the stage. The lines for the Prince were much longer than for the Princess. I was amazed that Soon-Bok had found the time to memorize them so perfectly. It was good that he could recite his lines so easily, but I was afraid he was rushing. Compared to Chang Kil-Ja's Princess, he showed neither emotion nor expressiveness, rather giving an impression of reading the lines off from the Korean Reader. Next was Young-Soo. His carriage on the platform was much calmer. He was great with the first few lines, but stumbled through the rest of his part. Each time he got stuck, the principal prompted him, but he got so flustered that he made a muddle out of the whole thing. Jeers and snickers were audible from around the stove. Almost crying, Young-Soo blushed as he stepped down off the platform, and then offered excuses to the teachers.

"Sir, I did know it all by heart, but it was so noisy and . . . ."

The teacher merely nodded, smiling. But the kids, upon hearing Young-Soo's excuse, laughed at him.

"Hey, everybody be quiet! Young-Soo's getting lost!" Someone said out loud, and the class then indeed was noisy.

At the teacher's call for silence, the group settled down. Then the teacher, after motioning with his chin for Young-Soo to return to his seat, stepped on the platform. As always, he began with stern voice,

"Here in front of you, I've decided the persons for the leading roles in the play you'll be performing."

Suddenly silence reigned in the room. A frightful animosity glowed in Gop-Soon's eyes as she glared at

Chang Kil-Ja, who was sitting with her face lowered.
"Soon-Bok will play the role of the Prince...."
Here he stopped, and looked us over before going on,
    "And for the role of the Princess, we've chosen
Chang Kil-Ja."
At this, a sharp, shrill voice rang out,
    "Sir!"
All our eyes converged on the source of the sound. Staring straight into the teacher's eyes, Gop-Soon stood up.
    "Sir, I didn't leave out or forget any of the lines like
Young-Soo did."
Gop-Soon, though daring, must have been somewhat embarrassed, for she was blushing as red as a beet. The teacher, stern until then, smiled benignly, with a grin not entirely free of awkwardness. But the children began to react. They all started banging the desks or stamping on the floor. I was among the loudest.
    "Sit down! Get lost!"
    "Shut up!"
Gop-Soon, until then impertinent, was completely dejected and collapsed back onto her seat at such a hostile reaction from her peers.
    "It's true that Gop-Soon memorized her lines perfectly, and her enunciation was clear. Still, Chang Kil-Ja was as good as Gop-Soon, and was better at expressing emotions with gestures. That's why we've selected Chang Kil-Ja."
The teacher explained the grounds for the final decision, but Gop-Soon still wouldn't accept it. As for Chang Kil-Ja, even after the announcement, she showed no trace of pride and still kept her head hanging down. The choice was completely sealed when the two who lost out on the leading roles were assigned other

roles to play.

No one planted the idea in my head, but I started to clap. The others began clapping along with me, and even the female teacher joined in the applause, showing her satisfaction with the results. Although the cast had been finalized, for a while we weren't able to practice the play in its entirety. Gop-Soon was given a fancy role, the Queen of Koguryo, but her pride must have been devastated by the loss of the Princess role, for she didn't come to school for several days. Then a rumor circulated that the role of the Queen would be given to someone else if she didn't show up soon. After that, she came back to school and joined in the rehearsals with the rest of us.

The friendship between Gop-Soon and Chang Kil-Ja was completely severed because of the casting contest. Gop-Soon openly displayed her hatred of Chang Kil-Ja. There could have been many ugly clashes if not for Chang Kil-Ja's patience and the general attitude of the class. Throughout the rehearsals I had many chances to observe that both Chang Kil-Ja and Gop-Soon were secret admirers of Soon-Bok. Gop-Soon was always aggressive and blunt, but Chang Kil-Ja's nature was indirect and patient. These kinds of interactions went far to help our play turn out successfully.

The agony of the Princess who had to burn the magic drum, and the fateful love which bound her to do the act... these passions couldn't have moved us without good acting. Chang Kil-Ja's performance as the Princess was excellent, and Soon-Bok was just as fine as the Prince. Thus, it wasn't surprising that Gop-Soon found it hard to look at them with much affection. Gop-Soon's jealousy, her obvious envy, helped move Soon-Bok to play his role closer to perfection.

On the day of the Arts Festival, the parents fought over the seats in the front row. A black curtain had been hung on the stage, which was a graduation present from the school alumni. As the woman teacher played organ music, the curtain slowly rose.

As the Prince's servant, I went out on stage early. Prince Ho-Dong looked magnificient in his ancient royal robe. Following behind him, I couldn't help hesitating a couple of times. Each time, our teacher, who was directing our every move from backstage, warned me in a whisper,

"Servant, follow a step closer behind the Prince!"

I had to pull myself together. I was distracted about my wretched appearance, and because I wanted to find out where my mother and father were sitting. Soon the Prince and I encountered the King of Nang-Nang Kingdom, who was walking toward us from the other side of the stage. The Prince, to whom the King took a liking at first sight, was invited to the Nang-Nang Palace.

Compared to the austere palace of Koguryo, the Nang-Nang Palace was magnificient and full of splendor. That was where the dream-like love between Prince Ho-Dong and Princess Nang-Nang first caught flame, and also where the heartrending farewell unfolded. Among the spectators who had witnessed the growth of their sweet love, some were now weeping at the cruel and unexpected separation. As I followed the Prince around, I was more interested in the audience than in what was happening on the stage.

The teachers, who in rehearsals were never satisfied with our performance, were now all smiles. Yet, I still vividly remember the way Gop-Soon waited backstage for the play to end, never once smiling, and a cold, bitter sneer frozen in her eyes.

Having returned to his native realm, Prince Ho-Dong had an ambition transcending his love for the Princess. To further his plan, he dispatched a messenger to the Nang-Nang Palace. The consternation after the arrival of the Prince's message, and the frightful trauma ensuing from it... the audience was drawn into the portrayal of the Princess and seemed to have even forgotten to breathe. Should she follow her beloved, deceiving her father, the King, and betraying her country? The Princess' agonizing trauma was so superbly acted that the audience was dragged into it without being allowed a moment for reflection.

I was sitting next to Soon-Bok, the Prince. He hung his head as if it pained him to cause any suffering to her even in the imaginary world of a play. Resigned, the Princess approached the Pavilion, and the stage lights dimmed as a special effect sent up a torch flaming into the air. By then a commotion was heard in the audience. But the stage was soon lighted again.

Several times, messages were delivered to the Nang-Nang King telling of an invasion by the Koguryo army of his realm. But the drum in the Pavilion made no sound as it always did at the approach of an enemy. The King's face grew distorted with rage. He learned what the Princess had done, and according to the law of the Kingdom condemned her, his own flesh and blood, to the scaffold. He then led his army in silence to face his foe.

With the capture of the Nang-Nang Palace, Prince Ho-Dong brought a vast land and population under his power, but having lost the most precious thing in his life, he had been transformed into a different man. Instead of elation, his heart was clouded with resurgent sorrow. With his servant at his side, he stood forlornly in the Palace, and spoke a grievous lament,

"I have lost what is more precious than a King's prerogative, my poor Princess who was so wise. Blinded by lust for fertile land and imperium, I have lost my love."

The Prince, abandoning himself to grief, looked quite beside himself.

The scene was then changed, and seated on the stage were the King and Queen of Koguryo. The King praised the Prince for his distinguished victory, and exhibited his deep trust in him. But the Queen, whose son Prince Ho-Dong was not, was jealous of the Prince's achievement. At first, the King closed his ears to the Queen's fabricated accusations of the Prince. But, since there's no tree that won't fall if you keep on chopping, the King in the end gave credence to the Queen's calumny.

Engulfed in sorrow at the loss of the Princess, the Prince ignored the false charges levelled at him, but he forsaw the decline of the Kingdom and what it might mean for him. So he resolved to kill himself.

"What paltry excuses do I need now to defend myself? The Queen is mother of the land. It is the duty of a son to accept the imputation, and not witness the suffering of the King by revealing the Queen's falseness."

The Prince unsheathed the sword at his side and pierced his own neck. I, his servant, stood beside him like a scarecrow as the curtain slowly fell, with a dirge-like chorus in the background.

Was the Prince, who betrayed the Princess, destined by a wretched fate to betray himself in the end?

After leaving Kil-Nam and his mother at their place, I took a walk in the thick fog, reminiscing about this and that episode during our own Arts Festival years earlier. As my vision grew dim in the fog, so did my memory in the waters of time, and recalling those fading events brought me both a quiet joy and sadness.

After the mother and child went in their house, I couldn't go directly home, so I mounted the hill behind the rye field where we used to climb in the old days. In the darkness no sounds of mountain birds, let alone of humans, were to be heard. I picked up my gait as though heading toward a place where someone awaited me. Then I would suddenly stop, once more lost in memories of a remote past.

The servant of Prince Ho-Dong... everyone had at least a few lines as they walked back and forth on the stage, everyone except the Prince's servant who followed the Prince without uttering a single word, like a mime. A mere servant who could only stand there dumbstruck even when his master stabbed himself to death... of course, there was no stage direction telling me to interfere with the suicide, yet would a faithful servant of the Prince simply watch him die? I, ordered to stand still like a scarecrow... how the audience must have loathed me.... So much time had passed that my recollection of it was dim, still I was overwhelmed with the same shame I had felt while standing out there on the stage. I couldn't drown myself indefinitely in that shame, and the sobering thought that next filled my head brought a different anxiety. That the servant was unresponsive to the Prince's death was a fault neither of the dramatist nor of the director, but rather a prophesy that forwarned me of days to come. Just as I was a mere spectator of the Prince's death, did I not simply sit back and watch Soon-Bok die? Like thunder echoing through black clouds, the bolting of such thoughts to and fro made me tremble so with fear and dread that I could no longer stand still. I, who had been unable to tell anyone of Soon-Bok's death, seemed doomed to play the tragic role in a ghastly pantomime, as sure as I was cast as the servant in that play. A servant destined to trail the Prince like a scarecrow... what should this servant now do for Kil-Nam and his mother, what help could a pantomime hero offer to them? Was I to remain indifferent even to them? They and I who had lost everying.... As I walked down the hill, my back was drenched with sweat.

I saw a light on in her house. My heart drew me to the light, but I had to turn away. The only sound I could hear was the waves breaking, and the stepping stone was buried in the night. What new tragedy could the village have in store to make the sea flail so in the darkness?

"Dear God!"

Not a star was visible in the sky. Even so, I had only the heavens to empty my heart into.

"Let all the misfortunes of the village be mine alone."

It was only much later that I found myself looking up at the starless sky. Never had I felt more despondent about life and death.

Back when I was a Marine... if I hadn't struggled against the tide after our boat capsized, then I wouldn't be dragging my life out and suffering this way... but, how desperately I fought then against the onslaught of death, how I thirsted for life.... What, then, was my desire? For the first time, I intensely felt the loneliness of the stepping stone that stood there in the rain and wind year after year. As I had shrieked at the sky, unless I could take everyone's misfortunes on my own shoulders, I wouldn't be able to abandon myself.

Remembrances of the Arts Festival were pleasant enough, yet the sentiment had somehow changed to a sadness tolling our destinies. The love between Prince Ho-Dong and Princess Nang-Nang didn't end with the play, it led to love between Soon-Bok and Chang Kil-Ja, leaving a legacy of stories revolving around the stepping stone.

Three years after the Arts Festival... those three years, for me, were a time of suffering and depression, of an incessant longing to leave the village behind. But they must have been the happiest, most blissful years for Soon-Bok. He was the only person I knew able to pacify my troubled soul and he persuaded me to stay.

It was a sunny day in the budding spring without a trace of the barren mood of the winter days just passed. I still recall the festive atmosphere in our village that week when Soon-Bok went to the junction on a horse borrowed from the mill owner and Chang Kil-Ja came down to our village on her wedding palanquin. Everyone in the village was feeling gay and festive but somehow Sang-Woon and I felt forlorn and defeated, like outcastes from our own village. In order to overcome that mood, Sang-Woon and I drank liquor until our eyes were bloodshot, but sadly enough, the more we drank, the clearer we thought.

Soon-Bok and Kil-Ja were the happiest couple in the village. When we returned to shore late, Kil-Ja was always out on the quay to meet her husband. On those nights, Sang-Woon and I would take a walk along the hillside, feeling an indescribable emptiness. The warm lights coming from Soon-Bok's house were especially exasperating. That light was, in a way, a beacon of their love. We used to imagine the young newlyweds sitting side by side beneath that light, sharing love and happiness together. On those nights I was plagued by insomnia.

This evening I saw the lights in Kil-Nam's house. As I used to long ago, I took a walk alone in the dark. Tonight also, like in the old days, I would probably spend a sleepless night. I stood in the midst of the same village, the same night, and same stream of time, yet I found it impossible to survive in the time flown by.

What had time left us? What had time taken from us?

Relics

"Soon-Bok, you should remarry."
I said casually to Soon-Bok, a few days before his death.

"I married once, so this time it will be a remarriage. A remarriage. I've made up my mind to remarry the sea."
Considering his slow speech and the repetition of the word "remarriage", he must have deliberated somewhat before replying, though I didn't notice at the time. Uncertain how to react to his answer, I didn't urge him any further. I just looked at him and smiled. I

was later tormented by the idea that he must then have already envisaged his own death.

The friendship among the three of us, as well as the dream we shared that used to bring us ecstasy, were over. But, the remembrance and the reality before my eyes were still in a state of confusion.

After the burial, I had to deal with the things he left behind. Nothing valuable to speak of. On the boat there were assorted utensils, and in the house which was about ready to be condemned, there was the summer Marine uniform he wore the day he returned home.

The uniform was burned so he could wear it on his way to the underworld, in accordance with a traditional village custom, but I found a little notebook in one of his pockets. Why I didn't burn it too, I still don't know. I kept the little book for a few days before I read it. Very few entries about life in the service, it was mostly a record of his life after discharge. The letters were as small as sesame seeds, and the grammar was often incomprehensible. First, I had to reorganize the little diary. But what was I to do with it afterwards? Give it to Soon-Bok's wife? Or should I let Kil-Nam have it when he grew up? I didn't know what good it would do for Soon-Bok's wife, or whether this sole legacy would be of any use to an adult Kil-Nam. But then what right did I have to keep Soon-Bok's secrets all to myself?

195x

The foreboding I felt as I traveled the road home turned out to be right. Before my homecoming, I saw many cities in ruins. Each time I felt deeply the extent

of horror and tragedy brought by the thoughtless destruction. Compared to those cities, my village seemed
to have preserved much of its old character. The waves,
the wind and the village were still the same. But the
desolation and loneliness passing through my soul were
worse than anything I ever felt at the sight of a demolished city. Nothing is left for me but the sense of loss.
Time ages everything, and a mind no longer youthful is
no better than a wasteland.

The enthusiasm that was mine when I departed to
join the Marine Corps was gone forever. I was told that
Sang-Woon was killed in action on the East Sea, and
that Young-Keun had not yet returned. I met a few
friends who made it home before me. One thing I felt
deeply was doubt about the meaning of my military
years. Protector of the nation, the bulwark of the nation... those were words I had heard too many times.
That was why I had not a moment of rest at the front,
always driven to prove myself worthy to be a proud son
of our nation. Now that I am back home, I can't help
but indulge in doubts about what I'd done. What had I
done as a soldier, a bulwark, to protect the nation and
my village? Now I saw only cities in ruins and a village
in decline... wasn't it true that I fought more to preserve my own life than to protect my country? Instead
of joy at my safe return, I felt only resentment that I
had not added one more anonymous grave in some far
away valley. To me, a village deprived of its youth was
no better than a tomb, without hopes or dreams. But I
didn't want to regard it as a curse for it was my own
village.

What had snatched the youth from our village?
What had altered our village? I wondered what my

comrades found, saw and felt when they returned to
their villages? Like a wind, the war had blown everything away. But now that the war had hidden its tail
under the grand "truce", against what do we fight to
seek revenge? To calm myself down and to restore
some order to my life, I had to rest for several days like
a man just emerging from fever.

All the dreams the three of us had cherished were
now forever dispersed like washed out waves. All the
same, I had to consider myself lucky for not having lost
those memories. Still, everything around me was too
empty for me to go on living on memories alone.

The village seemed to be hiding something from me.
I had a brief stay in the village, trying to figure it out,
but in vain. Mother had passed away, but I couldn't
locate her grave. My in-laws' house at the junction was
occupied by some refugees. They told me that my in-
laws had moved to Incheon. I also heard that my wife
might have gone with her family. Some young women
in the village, Young-Keun's father said, disappeared
after a foreign unit was stationed in our village. A
rumor that Gop-Soon had left with the foreigners still
lingered on the lips of the villagers like a legend, but I
heard not a word about my wife.

When I first enlisted, I didn't have a moment of
leisure to write letters, nor had she expected it from
me. What caused us to go on living without knowing
whether the other was alive or dead? Feelings that
once were so intense and full of life now served to make
the void even emptier. I took a walk near the bushes
where we used to catch meadow buntings, and along
the cliff near the stepping stone where Kil-Ja, still a
maiden, and I had shared our great hopes. We were a

boy and a girl who were then three years away from marriage. Our love, our promises and our marriage were as strong as the waves breaking on the cliff, and even now they were more substantial than the scattering foam. There was always our faith that formed the very heart of it all. I mean faith not so much in terms of trust and confidence shared between people, but a pledge linking two souls. Even at my most miserable, I could always find happiness in that pledge.

Now that I'm back home, why this malaise? Certainly it's not the anxiety of loneliness. It is distress coming from a sense of loss. What have I lost? Have I even lost her? Even if I haven't lost her, if she was taken away from me, the loss is the same. A rumor in the village had her seen in Incheon with our baby on her back... but more than that I couldn't root out. Even if it was a mere rumor, my joy when I first heard it was beyond telling. Having had everything taken from me, that I was blessed with such news seemed quite significant to me. Although it was just hearsay, it gave me untold courage.

I haven't actually lost her, I just haven't had a chance to find her yet. I have to hurry and get that chance. One thing I felt ashamed about even when feeling that extreme malaise was that in my mind I wasn't really ready for her. As I prepared to go off and seize the chance to look for her, my heart was full, and I felt as exultant as when the three of us first put out to sea years ago. The nameless dread that weighed on my mind was like the cumulus clouds that suggested fantastic dreams as we watched them float over the far horizon.

That night, I rummaged through the memories I'd

accumulated, like an old antique collector, who'd spent his life caressing valuable items, reliving his past finds. While an old man like that seeks meaning in tangible objects, I try to resurrect the ethereal dreams of a former life. Never again would she cast herself on the horns of another dilemma by burning a drum, nor would she damn herself out of self-pity... my wife avowed. Actually, they were the words of Chang Kil-Ja as a girl. After the Arts Festival, our relationship rapidly progressed, and we used to love to sit on the hill and watch the Milky Way, conversing on such topics. What touched me most was not talk of the Arts Festival, but recollections of the first adventure when we three boys ventured out to sea.

We'd had no plan in mind when we put out to sea on that boat. It was an entirely spontaneous urge, but our surroundings forced us to bestow a profound object on it. Somehow I felt embarrassed to say it was a purposeless journey, so without a second thought, I blurted out,

"We were trying to find Iyŏ Island."

She must have been amazed by my wild answer. Upon realizing that my response was foolish, I regretted that Sang-Woon and Young-Keun would be connected with it. She was in my grade, but life in town seemed to have made her more mature.

"I don't imagine Iyŏ Island out in the sea."

Her eyes were brighter than the stars, and her voice most passionate.

"Then where?"

I asked her, my eyes riveted on her continuously.

"I think Iyŏ Island is right here, this very spot, don't

you? I mean, this hill and this stepping stone where we now sit."

Unable to reply, I held her tight in my arms. The realization struck me that Iyŏ Island, for which our ancestors searched, and which the villagers today incessantly seek, even in their dreams, was not an island out in the sea but a place in our own hearts, right in our midst. Not surprisingly, the very idea kept me wide awake that whole night long. At last, I saw that the war and the times weren't to blame, that it was I who'd been oblivious of the paradise, Iyŏ Island, that lay before me in my heart, and now was missing from our village. As our ancestors set sail over the sea in search of Iyŏ Island, now I must depart in search of my wife, the Iyŏ Island of my soul. As long as my wife, our memories and I still live, no matter how barren and dismal our village may have become, we can make it into a springtime paradise again, graced with peach and apricot blossoms.

Having read this journal of his, I could roughly gather what must've gone through Soon-Bok's mind after his return home. But by the time I came back, he was already a hardened man who'd turned his back on terra firma. If only he had divulged a single word about his search for his wife, I never would have dreamt of committing such a horrible blunder. Our life wasn't that bad, and it wasn't for the money that we resorted to that dirty business. The war had taken everything from us, teaching by deprivation the value of material things. Soon-Bok sometimes spoke of the miserable state of our village, but I know now he meant something more than the rundown appearance of the place.

The whole nation had lost a generation, and so did our village. The greediness of old age and a mounting anxiety contributed to the sterility of our village, thrusting people into the throes of solitude and despair. Soon-Bok's search for his wife, the Iyŏ Island of his soul, was in a way a struggle to free himself from this prison as well as a desperate attempt to save his home. The lost generation was the missing pillar that would have been there to work at sustaining the order and well-being of the community.

After reading the first page of the diary, I went through a long period of reflection and self-reproach before recovering my lost self, and once more I was reminded of the unspeakable loneliness of the self. Hardened hearts, vicious minds, shattered morals, decrepit religion, corrupted souls...stranded in such surroundings and condemned to solitude, how was I to build a new Iyŏ Island? As Soon-Bok's unquiet mind couldn't rest the night before he was to embark on his search for the Iyŏ Island of his soul, I, too, spent the night sleepless, hearkening at the surging waves and peering into the darkness.

195x

From the outset my trip was an adventure, but it could never equal our first journey out to sea in search of that fabulous dream. I had to exercise patience and discretion at all times even though I was in a rapture of delight. I was like an alpinist who feels an uncontrollable surge of joy as he moves towards the main peak, and yet has to concentrate on every step he takes with the utmost care.

I can't deny that I benefited from social contacts on this trip. But those gains invariably hurt my pride. If I may exaggerate, people's lack of kindness makes it a completely different world. It is something more than just some postwar eccentricity. While the war was going on, there were still rights and duties we could claim. But the war closed with a truce. What, now, are we entitled to? Our rights and duties all relate back to the days before the war. In other words, we have the same rights and duties as other citizens. All the human interactions I witnessed seemed a mixture of irreversible change, restorable relations and rejection of tradition. That is why I consider acts of deference as a humiliation, as robbing me of my pride.

On the train, I carefully watched my fellow soldiers. I saw a cold discontent on their faces. What was the source of their wooden expressions, of their chill, of their evident dread? The uncertainty I had to face upon returning home, the humiliations endured during this trip . . . were these what had hardened them so? Their coldness and hostility showed the disgracefulness of their past conduct. What generated our mistrust, and what had evoked the shameful behavior? Even at the front we couldn't ignore its existence, but we felt some consolation in our belief that it was, after all, only one side, and not everything.

Until now we've been practically color blind. Color blind in the sense of only being able to see one color. But then our vision began to return. Like eyes first discerning black and white, recovery of our sight has made us sensitive to criticism. That was the way my eyes brought me awareness and sadness.

I was about to leave Taegu Station. At first I

couldn't believe my ears when I heard that voice, much too dry for a conductor's. Soon my doubt had become fury. I turned to face him, but everyone seemed to be laughing at me. As if already acknowledging my defeat, I closed my eyes to repress the fury. Perhaps it was to avoid the jeering looks rather than to control my rage. But I'll never forget the medal on his chest that I glimpsed as I rotated my head. The fiery fury was gone, and the next moment I was flustered to find myself on the verge of tears.

My comrade from the old days, now a disabled veteran . . . an honorable designation, like the medal on his chest. I put elbows on my knees and covered my face with both palms. How noble our pride once was! What deprived us of that pride, a pride preferring death to surrender into the hands of the enemy? What he now shouted was no appeal to the nation or to his compatriots. He was merely a pitiful beggar, relying on the cheapest sentimentality.

What we expected when we left the service wasn't that kind of pity. We hoped for the life we had earned by accepting and discharging our duties. But we lost life. Having spent the most precious, resilient years of our lives in the war, we became lame horses never to be needed again. Still, we have dreams of the old days when we ran at a full gallop with riders on our backs.

How long must we see our pride abused to gain pity? And what comes next when the pride and pity both run out? The hands covering my face were damp with cold sweat. The souls of my comrades who sacrificed themselves to history and now lay sleeping in nameless valleys, and those friends of mine who peddle their pride, medals hanging on their chests . . . shouldn't we do something for the history of our nation?

Even in my pain and sorrow, I never lost myself. My heart was always filled with hope for the future, because I had memories, Iyŏ Island and a wife I had to find.

The streets of Incheon seemed utterly changed. Even the looks on the faces of passers-by were different. The dreadful fear they revealed as they traveled south- wards to seek refuge was now gone, but a true sense of relief was not yet visible. Buying and selling no longer proceeded according to the principle of supply and de- mand, but primarily as dictated by sheer greed. For four days I swam through the stream of those un- familiar faces to look for the only face I knew. It was as hard as picking out gold dust from a sand dune. Worn out, my only hope was to rely on a chance meeting. I was walking the streets, praying for such a coincidence, when I spotted Gop-Soon. I recognized her at once, but her fancy dress made me hesitant to speak to her. She must also have recognized me, for she looked back several times as she walked on ahead of me.

I don't remember who spoke first, but somehow we found ourselves facing each other in the middle of the street. At one glance I could tell everything about her life. In the old days she always had jealousy and resent- ment in her eyes, but today I saw in them a certain dis- dain. It was a wonder that she hadn't just ignored me, and that she actually had stopped for me. She showed no recollection of the stepping stone village, and said not a word about it. After waiting for an improbable encounter, I was extremely glad to have run into her. She told me an unaccountable story about my wife that

left me no room to dwell on anything else for a long
while. After she left, I had an uncanny ache in my
darkening heart as I walked along the street. Only
much later did I realize why she had compulsively
stopped. Only then did I understand the disdain in her
eyes. The little she told me was meant not only to
elevate herself but also to mock Kil-Ja, my wife. She
said she saw Kil-Ja with a grown child, but that she
had left for Seoul because business was bad in Incheon
when you had a son that size . . . what business? An unnecessary question, for I could easily guess the whole
situation from Gop-Soon's tone of voice. Still I couldn't
allow myself to believe her words. It was true that we
had had our spats in the old days, but did that give her
the right to torment my soul? I looked back at the
street she had walked down, but she was already gone.
I couldn't move a step nor could I stop and sit. I stood
there like a statue. What had she meant by "business"
and a "grown child"? When I learned in the village that
she had a child, what joy and hope I felt for my own
flesh and blood! But why do I now feel such crushing
sorrow, fear and injustice in my head about this same
child? What cause have I to curse an unknown life,
when I haven't yet abandoned hope that my wife will
be mine again? Jealousy is love in excess, maybe
jealousy is just an ugly face of love.

Once in Seoul, I could only wander aimlessly in the
night streets. The nightlife in Seoul was too ex-
travagant for a city that had just emerged from a war.
New buildings were rising on demolished sites. Deep in
an alley, between the high-rise buildings, surrounded
by a stone wall, was the Royal Sanctuary where generations of kings had been buried in peace. This was an

area called "Jongsam", a notorious red light district. A quiet alley by day, boasting the ancient red and blue Shrine, a glorious past of Kingdoms gone by, suddenly, with the fall of night, is transformed into a fabulous world, heavily ornamented with flowers of sin. The night street where flames of passion burn and die.... For days and nights I wandered through the same alleys. They were interwoven like a spiderweb, packed with tiny buildings, but I remember each alley and house in the area. I wandered so long and became completely familiar with the area, but in no alley and under no eaves did I ever find the familiar face. When I left the dark alleys, pushing aside persistent temptations of young women, I felt my empty heart grow frigid as I gazed up at the starless night. It was pointless to ask myself where the emptiness came from, for, plagued with restlessness, I was unable to come up with a single word of reassurance.

The waves of war had wrecked the ark of our once peaceful family. And I stood in that alley a lost man, trying to save the woman who used to share that ark with me, I saw only too many of those women circling about the street. Still, in order to rescue someone, shouldn't I be out on the sea and not up on the mountain top hoping for a preposterous miracle? No matter how severe the shock had been or how terrible the damage of the storm, my wife would never abandon herself to drift on the tide of fallen women. Then, why was I looking for her here, and what made me doubt my wife?

Did I believe the rumors in the village and Gop-Soon's chatter? That I had so thoroughly scoured the vicinity of the Sanctuary was undeniable proof that, consciously or not, I had no faith in my wife. Until then I was the one shocked and dismayed at the drastic change in the world around me. Perhaps I believed I was the only one left unchanged. But I finally realized that it wasn't the world but myself that had changed. The war had robbed me of the most precious thing in my heart. There was no other explanation for my mistrust of my wife.

That night I stayed at an unlicensed inn near the station. For fifty hwan one could spend the night in wood-paneled inn, a bohemian heaven.

Where next? Now that I had lost the last thread of hope, my despair was without bounds. My mind, overcome by grief, was incapable of decision. During the day I worked as a porter at the station or in the market, and when twilight began to fall, I rushed back to the red light district.

What meaning did that existence have, and what did I gain from it? Reflection was torment, still I couldn't resolve to return to my village. So, my life fell into the routine of hanging about the station or the market place to earn enough to fill my empty stomach and then go back to the inn to sleep.

I always ate breakfast and supper at the same restaurant, also an underground place, near the inn. I became one of their regular customers. Mostly laborers frequented the place. The coarse edge of their dialect, their gloomy expressions, the signs of malnutrition on their faces, and the unsettled atmosphere with an aroma of gunpowder, all noxious remnants of the war. Everyone there downed a glass of wine with relish before eating. I never cared for wine, so I usually sat by myself to one side of the crowd. A place where everything was valued in terms of cash was bound to see lots of fights. Dead sober, I listened to them exchanging words in drunken voices. Having no place to go, even that place was a consolation to me.

Breakfast came very early and supper late for me. So it was well toward evening when I met the woman. We ran into one another once a day on average. I thought she was a young woman working at the restaurant. That was why I didn't hesitate to ask,

"Could I have some more hot soup, please?"

I saw her grow a little bit flustered at being so addressed. Then she called out to the proprietress in a familiar tone,

"Granny, please give some more soup to this customer."

I blushed before apologizing, but I suppose my blunder was the basis of our acquaintance. After this misstep, I began to become more and more interested in her.

For some reason it had been a very profitable day. So I went to the restaurant, our evening gathering place, earlier than usual. Due to the hour there weren't too many customers yet. Business being slow the granny and the chore girl were both resting on a wooden bench.

"Wouldn't it be nice to sell a glass of wine!"

At such remark from the owner of the place, a joke on my being a teetotaller, I felt like drinking that night.

"Well, let me be the first lucky break of your business."

As soon as I said it, the granny and the chore girl looked at me in amazement. I thought their reaction funny but also felt embarrassed somehow. I urged them to bring me a drink, for they seemed to think I was just offering a retort to their joke. After drinking a couple of glasses by myself, I offered a glass to granny. She was an old hag who probably swilled wine like water, but I hadn't actually seen her drinking before. So, I wasn't quite sure she would drink, but I offered it all the same.

"If you insist...."

Without a hint of hesitation, she moved over beside me and took the offered glass.

"Ah, granny, you can't start so early in the evening."

"Don't worry, little girl. It's not everyday I get a free drink. Better take it when I can get it."

I now saw that this old woman was unquestionably a wine lover. I was slightly drunk, and it fit with my mood. I don't know if it was the alcohol, but suddenly the woman I ran into every evening popped into my mind.

"I wonder what happened?"

I said it to myself, half expecting a response from the granny.

"What do you mean?"

The granny asked, after draining the glass in one gulp.

"I don't see any sign of her this evening."

"My, my."

I looked at her blankly.

"Since when did you fall head over heels in love with her? And all this time I thought you were a nice, quiet man. Watch out or you'll ruin your lot. Why don't you get married like you should?"

I blushed, and not because of the wine. The chore girl gave me a funny look and turned away. Just then the door opened and walked in the woman in question.

"Welcome, welcome!"

The garrulous granny was worse than usual, tugging the woman's sleeve and making her sit down beside her.

"Now, the person you've been longing to see is here, why don't you treat her to a nice dinner?"
I smiled, but didn't feel at all good, for the granny's remark was more of an insult than a good-natured rib. After that, there wasn't much I could do but sit there quietly.

"He's buying, so why not have a glass of wine, dear?"

"But I don't drink."
The granny emptied the glass herself.

As the door, inset with cloth instead of glass, gradually darkened, the little restaurant with three wooden tables began to bustle. Needless to say, I bought her dinner that evening. She came out of the restaurant behind me.

"I am sorry to have you spend so much money."
Her soft voice sounded especially gentle. I didn't know what to say, so I kept on walking ahead of her. It was a filthy alley but the darkness brought it a certain coziness. I looked at her, thinking about what the granny had said a while before. Her slightly pointed chin and sharp nose left a deep impression on me. For the first time, I wondered what kind of a woman she was.

"Do you live near here?"
I realized I was going in an entirely different direction from my inn. The time had come when I had to abandon all fancy ideas about her.

"My house is over there. Would you like to drop in?"
Like all the places on that hillside, her house was a shack, little better than a thatched hut.

Starting that evening, she and I saw each other fre-
quently. Soon afterwards I moved from my inn to her
place, and the meals we used to take at the unlicensed
restaurant she now prepared in her own kitchen. I
need not explain what this life was to me. Still, for the
few days I spent with her I could at least bury all my
wounds in oblivion. They were happy days for me, but
also days that seared an indelible remorse deep into my
heart, a remorse that will be there as long as I live.

During those happy days, her face helped me forget
the image of the wife I had so longed for, and I also
found, in her small child, a counterpart of the dream,
based on hearsay, of my own son. Like myself, she was
a woman who had lost everything in the war. The only
livelihood she had was the life of a prostitute in a
wooden shack patched together with bits of newspaper. Who made her wander on the street of no
return? But I had a new hope. My daily labor was no
longer only for shelter at an underground inn and
meals at an unlicensed restaurant. Though we woke up
and went to bed in a patched shack, our hope was
sacred. So I worked like two men, running like a
maniac all over the place. We had to pay the rent for
her place, and once we paid off the debts she owed to
her landlord we could live happily ever after. For me,
saving her was a compensation for losing my wife,
enabling me to justify myself as righteous.

That day, too, was a profitable day. Usually a porter
earns most in the early and late hours of the day, but
for some reason, before noon I had already made three
times more than I usually did in a whole day. It was a
rare boon, indeed. In view of my good luck, I decided
to go home early to have lunch with her. So I hurried

back, carrying a bagful of food I'd bought.

When I saw her son standing with his back to me, ignoring my approach, I thought his mother had scolded him. I called to him, but he was still sulking and didn't answer me. I opened the door, patting the little boy on the head.

I can't write down what I saw at that moment. I only remember that I dropped the bag, and hastily ran out of the alley with the child crying behind me.

All my dreams were again dissolved. Even the hate which once sent me flying into uncontrolled rages is now gone. If jealousy is an ugly face of love, so is hatred. What I hated wasn't her behavior. The rage was for love betrayed. But those feelings had left me long ago.

Like the quietly falling sleet that piles up in our stepping stone village under the thick fog, irrevocable remorse is silently coating my heart. Why did she sell her body in the broad daylight? That question remained in my heart without an answer. Once out on the street, she was drawn back to her prior habit, and I had lost a place to which I could return.

That was the last page of his diary. Having read it I could answer a couple of questions. After he came back from the service, Soon-Bok set off for Seoul with a hope, the same way we had gone to sea the first time. He probably didn't suffer much then because he was hopeful of recovering the sweet repose of his heart and had the ambition of regaining Iyŏ Island. But without any trace or scent it was impossible to recover the trail of lost happiness. On the turning wheel of history he must have despaired after trying to find himself, drifting along on the rough storm, clutching desperately at every piece of flotsam. Was it a dream of happiness, irrevocable and lost? Was it fate that imposed even greater hardships on him? His encounter with the woman, though like hitting a desert island after a long drift, became to him a materialization of all his hopes, a paradise of a little kingdom.

Come to think of it, the island Soon-Bok reached was already a paradise lost, but because the storm on which he had drifted was so rough, he was relieved to land anywhere, dreaming of a flower gracing a fig tree in the barren garden of Eden. Eve, tempted, was forgiven by Adam, but who could save an Eve who herself tempted the serpent? As Adam was cast out of Eden with a yoke on his back, Soon-Bok must have been driven to a new wandering by the most profound rage after losing even the mock paradise.

It wasn't written in his journal, but he must have come back to the village at the end of that wandering. Then why, after returning, did he spend the rest of his life on the boat? In search of an answer to this question, I read his diary again. The war took all his dreams from him, but it was apparent that he always held on to himself. It was only after he had lost himself, too, that he returned home to the village. Nothing could console or release him from his grief at losing himself. He was left with remorse, nothing more. Wasn't it that remorse that barred him from ever stepping on land again? Reading his journal the second time, I found myself reminiscing about the old days. Soon-Bok who was Prince Ho-Dong and Chang Kil-Ja Princess Nang-Nang... had we not been living the lives predestined for us from that moment? After betraying the princess, Prince Ho-Dong had no choice but to kill himself, and Soon-Bok, having lost himself and suffering from self-pity, could never find his wife. His simple passion, which told him he could never have her back, made him remain on the sea for the rest of his days. I suppose he was trying to recreate his lost Iyŏ Island on the horizon we, as boys, had once possessed. That was why the way he looked at the shore was so different from his attitude when facing the sea. His eyes shone when he held an oar or the boom, but a dark despair filled them whenever we headed toward the shore.

Why did Soon-Bok jump into the water that night? Was it, after all, my scheme that drove him to choose that way out? At the end of his long wanderings he was without memories, without Iyŏ Island, and only an un-fathomable despair awaited him. And even after his ill-starred affair, love for his wife still burned in his heart, making his despair deeper than even the deepest sea.

The world about me is completely washed out, with no room for any rearrangement. Our youth, never reaching full bloom, was prematurely buried. The only thing left was remembrance of our boyhood.

Reordering

It was several days after I buried Soon-Bok. As usual, I didn't feel like going out to sea in the morning. The mere thought of the sea and its surging waves made me sick. Only wine could soothe my mood. For three straight days, I gazed out on the sea with hazy, drunken eyes. The sound of waves, which always made my heart violently throb, now echoed like curses that had robbed me of everything. Was it possible that the cradle for all my dreams could turn overnight into a malevolent hell?

In the end, I have lost even the sea. A fisherman without the sea is like a farmer without land. I heard that the farmers who lost their land during the Japanese occupation moved to the far north or to Manchuria in search of new land. Where am I, who have lost the sea, to go?

I spent all day wandering the hills beyond the rye field where we used to romp about. The blue sky and the grass where we used to roll about were still there, like a dilapidated house or a discarded toy. But the surroundings were empty.

That day too, I came home late. My father must have known I was coming from the sound of my footsteps.

"Soon-Bok's wife is back, Soon-Bok's wife is. . . ."
I noticed someone had come to our place, but I only half believed my father's words even when I came face to face with Soon-Bok's wife under the eaves in the twilight. I was not quite sober, but the only change I could detect was that her face was a bit thinner than before. She had already heard everything about Soon-Bok from my father. At the sight of me, she turned around and wept quietly.

"This is Soon-Bok's son!"
Said my father, and only then I saw a little boy standing beside her. He was a spitting image of Soon-Bok when he was young. As I patted him on the head, he hung his head down and turned away.

I felt lost for a long time, like a man abruptly awakened from a dream. The appearance of Soon-Bok's wife and son brought a new wave to my otherwise uneventful life. It was more of a tragedy than a lost sorrow. What could I do? Submerged in remorse and disconcertment, I couldn't hold up my head. I regretted the tragedy I had irreversibly abetted. Captive to this regret, I had to listen to her tell me the story of the past years of her life. The enlistment of her husband, the stationing of foreign troops in the village, the catastrophe of losing her whole family in bombing on their way to take refuge, and after that she spent a long time moving about in search of her husband. Chinhae, Incheon, and other places. She had moved from place to place. Meanwhile, the little one on her back had grown enough to walk on his own, and she heard a rumor that her husband, who she thought had been killed in action, had returned home. That was when she hurried back to the village. But the sole light before her had already died down. Only despair and darkness were present at the reunion.

"I'll keep watch over the soul of my husband, bringing up this little one, his only gift."
She said in a low voice, the sleeping child on her lap. In the dark despair, I was deeply impressed by her strong will.

I was reordering the nets that I had abandoned for days.
"Uncle, what are you doing?"
"Um?"
I stopped and turned around. It was Soon-Bok's son.
"Got up early, didn't you?"

"Yes, I've been up for some time."
Born and raised in the war, but there was no trace of sorrow in Kil-Nam's eyes.
"Going out to sea?"
"Um."
As he watched me, I completed arranging the net.
"Uncle, take me with you, please."
"Have you eaten breakfast?"
"Yes. I ate early so I could go to sea with you."
Reflecting on the old days, I let him come on the boat as he wished.

While I steered, Kil-Nam sat at the prow of the boat watching the billowy sea. It was like the morning, so long ago, when the three of us put out to sea for the first time. In an attempt to subdue those sad and beautiful memories I closed my eyes.

"Uncle, where is Iyŏ Island?"
Applying full force to the oars, I looked at Kil-Nam. It wasn't Kil-Nam, but a young Soon-Bok with a burning thirst for adventure.

"Mother said father is gone to Iyŏ Island."
I could remain silent no longer.
"Iyŏ Island is far off beyond that horizon."
My voice trembled slightly. Peering at the horizon I'd indicated, Kil-Nam's face grew tense with excitement.

"Uncle, let's go to that island called Iyŏ Island."
"No, not yet. You have to grow up before we make the trip."
What a heartless answer that must have seemed. I had only myself to blame for having to stifle his only hope.

Sitting at the head of the boat and gazing at the horizon with cumulus clouds hanging over it, Kil-Nam seemed to be dreaming of some adventure of his own.

Once again I pulled the oars with all my strength. Was remote Iyŏ Island, the place where all our hope and happiness lay, after all, the only legacy bequeathed us by our ancestors in the stepping stone village?

I am the lonely watchman at the lighthouse guarding Iyŏ Island. Is it not an irony of fate that I will live on, guarding the beacon called Kil-Nam as an outsider, just like when I was a servant in a pantomime?